DOCUMENTS OF MODERN HISTORY

D0088590

General Editors:

A. G. Dickens

The Director, Institute of Historical Research, University of London

Alun Davies

Professor of Modern History, University College, Swansea

BISMARCK AND EUROPE

edited by

W. N. Medlicott

Emeritus Professor of International History,
University of London

and

Dorothy K. Coveney

Edward Arnold

© W. N. Medlicott and Dorothy K. Coveney 1971

First published 1971 by
Edward Arnold (Publishers) Ltd.,
41 Maddox Street,
London W1R 0AN

Clothbound edition ISBN: 0 7131 5601 5
Paperback edition ISBN: 0 7131 5602 3

Printed in Great Britain by
R. and R. Clark Ltd., Edinburgh

CONTENTS

ABBREVIATIONS

APP	*Die Auswärtige Politik Preussens 1858-1871* (Oldenburg, 1932 +)
BFSP	*British and Foreign State Papers*
Bismarck	Otto Eduard Leopold von Bismarck-Schönhausen, 1815-1898
Bonnin	*Bismarck and the Hohenzollern Candidature for the Spanish Throne. The Documents in the German Diplomatic Archives* (London, 1957)
DDF	*Documents Diplomatiques Français (1871-1914)*, first series (1871-1900) (Paris, 1929 +).
F. O.	Foreign Office
GMF	Microfilm copies of German Foreign Office documents, Public Record Office, London
GP	*Die Grosse Politik der Europäischen Kabinette 1871-1914* (Berlin, 1922 +), first series (1871-1890). ed. J. Lepsius and others
GW	*Bismarck: Die gesammelten Werke* (Berlin, 1923 +), ed. H. von Petersdorff and others
Hertslet	*The Map of Europe by Treaty* (London, 1875-1891, 4 vols), by Edward Hertslet
Jelavich	*Russia in the East 1876-1880 ... as seen through the Letters of A. G. Jomini to N. K. Giers* (Leiden, 1959), ed. Charles and Barbara Jelavich
OD	*Les origines diplomatiques de la guerre de 1870/71, Recueil de documents officiels* (Paris, 1910 +)
Pflanze	*Bismarck and the Development of Germany, The Period of Unification, 1815-1871* (Princeton, 1963), by Otto Pflanze
Pribram	*The Secret Treaties of Austria-Hungary 1879-1914*, by A. F. Pribram (Cambridge, Mass., 1920: English edition, ed. A. C. Coolidge)
RA	Royal archives, Windsor
R & R	*Bismarck, His Reflections and Reminiscences* (London, 1898)
Saburov	*The Saburov Memoirs or Bismarck and Russia* (Cambridge, 1929), by J. Y. Simpson
Schweinitz	*Denkwürdigkeiten des Botschafters General v. Schweinitz* (Berlin, 1927)
SR	*Slavonic and East European Review*
WSA	Wiener Staatsarchiv
Y.E.	Your Excellency

PREFACE

The purpose of this selection of documents is to illustrate the tactics and some of the arguments by which Bismarck brought Prussia to dominance in north Germany, and Germany to predominance in Europe. For reasons of space it is hardly possible to follow all the intricacies of the masterly negotiations which sometimes prove no more than his understanding of the virtues of patience. But the work does examine the problem of Bismarck's European relations in each of its successive phases, and it includes some representative examples of the reaction to Bismarck's policy and ideas of men and governments outside Germany.

The official documentation for the subject is abundant; much of it, although by no means all, has already been published. In the main publications there are, indeed, strange gaps. Ten volumes of *Die auswärtige Politik Preussens, 1858-1871*, were published between 1932 and 1945; they print Bismarck's diplomatic correspondence in the 1860s but with nothing for the periods April-July 1866 and February 1869 to 1871, the periods, that is, of Bismarck's two major wars. Its successor for the period 1871-90 is the first series of *Die Grosse Politik der europäischen Kabinette, 1871-1914*, six volumes published in 1922. This was admittedly a selection, but it is a far more rigorous one than many biographers of Bismarck seem to realize; it omitted, for example, most of the documents relating to the negotiation of Bismarck's secret treaties. These gaps can sometimes by filled by documents drawn from the archives of the German foreign office and of other governments, and by revelations which appear in the memoirs of Bismarck's contemporaries. The present selection draws on these sources, and includes some important, and hitherto unpublished, German, British, Austrian, and Russian material. All translations of extracts, except those quoted from English editions are by the editors.

Weybridge,   W.N.M.
December 1970   D.K.C.

ACKNOWLEDGMENTS

The editors and publisher wish to thank the following for their permission to use copyright material: Alfred Costes (**E11**(i),(iii), **H5**, **H12**, **I1**; Harvard University Press (**G7**, **G16**, **G21**, **I1**); Verlag von Reimar Hobbing (**D10**, **E2**, **F7**, **G3**); the Controller of Her Majesty's Stationery Office (**E3**(i), **F1**, **F15**(iii), **G2**, **I2**(i),(iii)); Macmillan (**J2**); the editor of *The Slavonic and East European Review* (**F10**); Gerhard Stalling Verlag (**B4**, **B6**, **D4**), and the Vienna State Archives (**F15**(i), **G6**, **G9**, **G11**, **G12**, **G12**(iv),(v), **I3**, **I16**, **I11**, **I13**). Extract **D1** from the Royal Archives appears by gracious permission of Her Majesty the Queen.

The editors would also like to thank Dr. S. C. Hunter for kindly supplying the transcripts used in extracts **H1** and **H2**.

INTRODUCTION

The clue to Bismarck's development is to be found partly in his personality, partly in the frustrations of Prussian politics in his early manhood. With splendid physique and a footing in both the bourgeois and Junker worlds through his parents, he made a somewhat undisciplined start in life as a junior civil servant and then spent some years restoring the fortunes of his family estates. At the same time he travelled a good deal in England, France, and elsewhere, and learned languages. Until his first encounters with political realities in 1847 at the age of 32 he displayed a certain scornful tolerance towards the liberal, nationalist, and cosmopolitan tendencies of the age (A,**1**). But during the 1848-9 revolutionary era he rapidly established a reputation as one of the most extreme opponents of a Germany united on a basis of liberal nationalism.

Undoubtedly his instinct for a dramatic role led him to flaunt this aggressively conservative attitude, and to call for the unimpaired maintenance of the rights of the aristocratic Prussian Junker class as the bulwark of the Hohenzollern dynasty. But by 1851 he could already see the possibilities of some different form of German unification in which Prussian power would be reinforced and dominant under the rule of its natural masters. His own arrogant self-confidence and eagerness for a commanding role made the achievement and maintenance of this dominance his lifework.

Unless the other great powers of Europe—Russia, France, Britain, and a little later Italy—chose to interfere, this problem would be one solely for the 39 states of the German Confederation (*der deutsche Bund*). Under the Federal Act of 1815 Austria, while possessing only one vote in the Federal Diet, presided and could count on the governments of the stronger minor German powers—such as Bavaria and Württemberg—in maintaining the independence of member states and resisting Prussian attempts to challenge Austria's very negative and obstructive leadership. But it was, in fact, always more than a merely German problem. Russia in particular felt responsibility for the preservation of the Concert of Europe and had exerted herself in 1850 to support the restoration of the Confederation after Austria had challenged the half-hearted attempt of King Frederick William IV of Prussia

1

and his advisers to set up a rival in the form of the Erfurt Union. Prussia's surrender had been registered in the Olmütz Punctation of 29 November 1850. Bismarck was a German nationalist only to the extent that he was prepared to mobilize nationalist sentiment in some circumstances in order to justify Prussia's role; and he did not regard this as a decisive weapon in the struggle. He relied far more on the ultimate sanction of Prussian arms and more immediately on diplomatic manoeuvres to isolate Austria within the European Concert.

The first section (A) of the documents prints examples of Bismarck's energetic representations on foreign policy to the Prussian government during the first phase of his public career in the eighteen fifties. As the Prussian ambassador to the German Confederation at Frankfurt he was even better placed than the politicians in Berlin to appreciate the indignities of Prussia's role at this period. His arguments for strengthening Prussia's international position by an ingenious policy of alliance failed to carry conviction, not because they were intellectually unconvincing but because he was urging action when political dynamism was at a discount. Prussia and the smaller German states were in a rather depressed and quiescent mood after the failure of the 1848-9 revolution and the re-establishment of Austrian ascendancy in the restored Confederation, and the Prussian government was content to keep out of trouble and to whittle away the liberal gains at home. All that Bismarck succeeded in doing at this period was to establish himself in the mind of the Regent, Prince William, who became king in 1861, as a masterful conservative extremist and trouble-shooter who should be called to office only in a case of dire emergency.

And yet Bismarck was not by temperament a war-lord with ever widening horizons of conquest.[1] The essential problem of Prussian or German foreign policy, as he saw it throughout his career, was that of seizing and maintaining a margin of advantage in European politics without having to pay a compensating price for doing so. This was partly because of his acute sense of Prussia's (and Germany's) relatively limited resources. In his first major utterance on attaining power in 1862 he talked of Prussia having to bear burdens too great for her frail body (B,3), and in his last, in the memoirs published after his death in 1898, he insisted that Germany's vulnerability meant that she must be 'appeased and peaceful', that she must not engage in preventive wars, and that she was 'the single great power in Europe which is not tempted by any objects which can only be attained by a successful

[1] Otto Pflanze, *Bismarck and the Development of Germany* (Princeton, 1963), pp. 89-92.

war' (J,7). The theme recurs constantly in his political conversations and writing. His skill in repeatedly denying any edge of advantage to others in the transactions of the sixties was due also, however, to a huckstering element in his diplomacy; he fiercely enjoyed having the best of a bargain, even on occasions when an inexpensive concession would have paid him well. As the years went on he was successful, disliked, and increasingly nerve-racked as he brooded over the jealousy and animosity, real or imagined, of thwarted allies, neighbours, and enemies.

The conditions of domestic deadlock which made a vigorous foreign policy useful as a distraction after 1862 also provided obstacles which had to be warily circumvented. The three main phases of crisis which occupied him during the sixties are the subject of the next three sections (B), (C), and (D).

One question that continually faces the student is the degree of premeditation in Bismarck's diplomacy. The picture of Bismarck assessing all eventualities amid the ever-denser blue cigar smoke during long contemplative evenings at Frankfurt is merely romantic, for while the broad objectives of Prussian national policy (as he saw them) were too familiar to need much pondering, opportunities for action would depend, as he knew well enough, on the chance moves or mistakes of other powers. They would also depend on the inclinations of his royal master. There is no reason to doubt the authenticity of his remarks to Disraeli in the summer of 1862 (B,2), but as a prophecy the programme did not go beyond the settlement of accounts with Austria and the minor German states. He did not make any reference to a future war with France or even a crisis with Denmark over the Schleswig-Holstein question. He showed increasing skill after the summer of 1863 in pursuing alternative policies simultaneously. He liked to have several paths before him and to be able to change from one to another as circumstances warranted. In the case of Austria the Gastein convention of August 1865 and the consideration of Anton von Gablenz's plans in the summer of 1866 kept open the faint possibility of agreement with her in case foreign intervention, the collapse of Habsburg resolution, or King William's conscience should rule out war. These ingenuities complicate the task of deciding his true purpose at any given point, for it is clearly unwise to assume that an eventual choice was predetermined, or that a rejected alternative had not served purposes of its own.

The complexity of the negotiations and subterranean bargaining involved in this sort of diplomacy could obviously have led to confusion

and disaster in less dexterous hands. Bismarck was already displaying
in the Danish negotiations of 1863-4 a remarkable degree of virtuosity
in this respect, and the ability to pursue his apparently conflicting ends
without prejudicing his final choice or just getting into a thorough
muddle. There were certainly occasions (as in the Polish crisis early in
1863, the War-in-Sight crisis in 1875, and the colonial issues in 1884)
when he acted irritably or impulsively and suffered rebuffs. These are,
indeed, frequent after 1871. They are a reminder that he was by nature
a violent and masterful man, whose patient adroitness when he chose
to apply it was a triumph of mind over impulse. His admirers have
produced some misleading diplomatic history by assuming his infallibility in all circumstances and then seeking by over-ingenious explanations to account for his less successful activities. The fact remains
that in the half-dozen great phases of political action when opportunity
and danger were equally balanced he did remain calculating and cool;
his timing was seldom at fault and it was his political opponents who
suffered disasters.

For these reasons, however, his statements have always to be read in
the light of the immediate effect which he wished to produce. He
prided himself on his ingenuity in telling the truth, in order when
necessary to deceive (J,7).[2] He also needed very able and obedient
servants in the foreign office and among the ambassadors, who would
accurately follow instructions without always understanding their
purpose. The Prussian diplomatic service had, however, many de-
ficiencies in 1862; the greater glamour of the military life and the
uninspiring quality of Prussian foreign policy since 1815 had had its
effect on the quality and ardour of the recruits. Bismarck gave great
attention to this problem, and his own successes in due course raised the
public standing of the service. He showed a preference for suitably
qualified military men; unlike the 'home-made' recruits from the
Prussian squirarchy they at least understood discipline (A,2). The
quality of the personnel gradually improved, and Bismarck was in-
sistent on businesslike procedure and objective reporting. Even the
admirable Schweinitz was warned to avoid sarcasm in his communications (D,10). Bismarck could deal fiercely on occasion with ambassadors who followed policies of their own. One of these was von
der Goltz in Paris (B,7). Bismarck did not finally assert his mastery
until the dismissal of another ambassador to Paris, Count Arnim, in
1874. One complication was that the ambassadors had direct access to
the King of Prussia.

[2] Cf Ludwig Reiners, *Bismarck* (Munich, 1958), i, 196-7.

It can of course be asked whether the diplomatic obstacles in Prussia's path in the sixties were as formidable as German publicists, if not Bismarck himself, have assumed. 'If he played his hand with great skill, it was a good one in the first place,' writes Professor W. E. Mosse. 'Neither British nor Russian statesmen felt the interests of their countries threatened by the consolidation of Germany.'[3] Bismarck's sanguine plans in the late fifties for alliance with France, and his conviction that Russia had disinterested herself in the defence of Germany against a French attack (A,7), show that he was not himself greatly concerned about the possibility of foreign interference with Prussian self-assertion in the German national movement. If it did take place, Austria would be more likely to suffer, for she had lost Russia's friendship in the Crimean war, and alienated France over her Italian policy, culminating in the 1859 war. After 1862 this basic alignment did not fundamentally change, and the assumption in Paris and St. Petersburg that Prussia would be no match for Austria in war reduced still further any likelihood of French or Russian alarm over, or armed intervention against, Prussia's forward plans.

But in any case, after the economically exhausting and morally discouraging Crimean episode and the further economic strain of the Polish crisis in 1863, Russia was in no mood to go to war with anyone if she could help it. She still desired to maintain in Germany the conservative governments, dynastic interests, and decentralized *Bund* which she had helped to restore at Olmütz, but she was not inclined to intervene except diplomatically. This governed her action in the Danish crisis in 1864, and although the tsar was at first painfully alarmed at the prospect of great changes after Sadowa he did not persist in his demand for a Congress in the face of Bismarck's fierce opposition. Russia's national interest pointed to the Near East as the true sphere for a forward policy if—sometime in the future—this became practicable. With the Crimean grouping (France, Britain, Austria, and Italy) tending to revive in the face of any such initiative, Russia moved warily and recognized Prussia as her sole potential ally, a view strengthened when the temporary Franco-Russian rapprochement of the post-Crimean years collapsed with French intervention in the Polish crisis of 1863.

It is true also that British opinion was well enough disposed in principle towards the advance of German nationalism, which satisfied liberal sympathy with people 'struggling to be free' in Italy, the

---

[3] W. E. Mosse, *The European Powers and the German Question, 1848-1871* (Cambridge, 1958), p. 372.

Balkans, Poland, and even—for a time—the Confederate states of North America. Political considerations complicated the issue, without destroying the basic British acceptance of unification. A united north German state would, it was (wrongly) assumed, be mainly Protestant, a natural ally or at any rate no natural enemy of Great Britain, and a likely counterpoise to France and Russia. Schleswig-Holstein was the only point at which a direct clash of interests between the two countries was threatened, and Palmerston's resistance to German nationalist attack on the duchies in 1849 did not signify disapproval of the nationalist movement itself. By 1864 the traditional English objections to the control of the entrance to the Baltic by a strong European power were felt to have lost much of their weight, and the forcefulness of Austro-Prussian action against Denmark annoyed the British government and British opinion without galvanizing them into action. Of the powers which had been so active in this issue from 1849 to 1852 France held back, and Russia was not prepared to intervene. The Anglo-French alliance had ceased to have meaning by 1863, and although it continued to have its advocates in London there seemed no compelling ground for abandoning the somewhat distrustful isolationism which British governments maintained towards the German question until 1870. It is evident, however, that Bismarck did not think of Britain as an enemy, but as a coy and patronizing friend whose alliance he sought from time to time.

Even in the case of France there was no implacable will to frustrate Prussian ambition. This was not due to any doubts about the threat to the European balance of power which would be created by a stronger Germany, whether led by Austria or Prussia, but rather to the tendency down to 1866 to undervalue Prussia as compared with Austria and to the many distractions, domestic and foreign, which Napoleon III had to face. He preferred to handle the German problem by skilful diplomacy, which generally meant a rather too obvious encouragement of Prussia at Austria's expense, and, if the post-1815 political deadlock of central Europe could not be perpetuated, the securing of safeguards and compensations for France. This was Napoleon's policy immediately after the surprise and shock of Sadowa, and it was entirely Bismarck's fault that no face-saving formula was found. Any hope of finding some such basis for permanent amiability rapidly receded. On both sides of the frontier emotional tension was building up during the next four years. Both governments understood the advantages of a military victory: each knew the cost of defeat.

The nightmare of coalitions against Germany, which was to disturb his sleep so often as Imperial Chancellor, was beginning to loom up in the advice which he received from other governments in April 1867 to behave reasonably towards France in the Luxemburg question. In short, Prussia was beginning to lose the freedom of manoeuvre resulting from her relative insignificance as a power before 1866. The frightening element in this bad dream was not so much that France would find strong allies as that Germany would come to depend on unreliable friends. His efforts at this time to improve relations with Austria, and to form an alliance with Britain on the basis of co-operation over Belgium and the eastern question, came to nothing. He secured a useful anti-Austrian arrangement with Russia in March 1868 (D,4), but on terms which were far from affording Russia the whole-hearted support in the east that was her price for permanent alliance.

The Prussian victory in 1870, like that of 1866, seemed abundant justification for a policy which would have been condemned as needlessly provocative and ineffectually calculating in the event of defeat. Sir Robert Morier, British minister to Stuttgart, who had prophesied before Sadowa (C,5) that this would be the case, completely accepted the new position of Germany in 1871 (D,11).

Certainly when Prussia's reasonable political and territorial objectives had all been attained, in his view, with the formation of the German Empire on 18 January 1871, he confined himself henceforth to the defence and internal improvement of his sated masterpiece. The first thing that must strike the student is the permanent atmosphere of crisis of his nineteen-year Chancellorship, which can only partially be explained by genuine fear of attack. The new empire, pressing against the frontiers of the three other strong continental powers, was undoubtedly vulnerable to attack and it went without saying that Germany's proved military superiority must be maintained: there were occasions therefore when publicity amounting even to war-mongering was needed to keep patriotic fervour alive and whip up electoral support for the regime and its military budget. There were, however, more genuine causes of tension.

One resulted from the growth after the seventies of expansionist aspirations which found their first outlet in the beginnings of the colonial movement and led on to the more exuberant calls for 'world-policy' under William II. And there was from the start a residue of unsatisfied German nationalist aspiration which accepted Bismarck's two forms of the *kleindeutsch* state in 1866 and 1871 as merely a brilliantly contrived instalment, to be followed by further accretions of

German power in Europe. These *grossdeutsch* nationalists had their counterparts in Austria, and were not silenced, although their appeal was weakened, by the Dual Alliance of 1879. As the years went by it could be seen that in the political climate of the new Germany apprehension was strangely mixed with arrogance; Germany was surrounded by jealous neighbours, but Bismarck himself, it was felt, had shown how to triumph by boldness and craft. As he became increasingly circumspect the younger generation of officers and officials became increasingly impatient. The eighties ended with much talk of the need for a preventive war with Russia.

A further source of tension was the existence of enemies, if not of the new Reich at least of its centralized direction, within the gates, each in the form of minorities looking elsewhere for support. In Alsace and Eastern Lorraine, annexed in 1871, France had a grievance so tangible and explicit as to rule out the hope of permanent reconciliation with Germany by any French government; Germany had a bad case which was merely advertised by such absurdities as Treitschke's remark that the misguided will of those Alsatians who preferred French rule should be ignored in favour of the pro-German inclinations of their ancestors. Bismarck admitted to the French envoy in August 1871 that the provinces were 'a Poland with France behind it'. Polish nationalism had worried him since 1863, and did not supply the automatic guarantee of conservative solidarity between the three empires that he would have liked. The Austrians favoured their Polish as against their Ruthenian subjects in Galicia and caused unfavourable comparisons with the condition of Prussia's Poles; there were elements in the Russian government which favoured a conciliatory policy based on the 1815 constitution. Above all there was a dangerous open military frontier, and Bismarck was periodically alarmed by Russian troop movements (always 'routine') and strategic railway building in the Russo-Polish areas. In the south-west the four states which had joined the empire in 1871 brought in a strong Catholic minority; it found vigorous spokesmen in the new Centre Party, favoured decentralization, looked (although not to the extent that Bismarck believed) to Rome for guidance, and had in the past played off Austrian against Prussian leadership. One might add a fourth minority problem in the north, for Austria could remind Bismarck of certain unfulfilled clauses of the treaty of Prague with regard to the Elbe duchies.

In the strictly diplomatic field after 1871 his main concern was the insoluble French problem and he was never completely satisfied with the system of alliances which he devised for her isolation. His uneasiness was shared by many of his compatriots, in so far as they under-stood the situation. The Three Emperors' League of 1872-3 was any-thing but a carte blanche permission to him to repress the French, who found a surprising amount of diplomatic support in the War-in-Sight crisis of 1875. Nor did it provide any help in his struggle with a new and elusive opponent, Pope Pius IX. The whole of the first five years of empire (1871-5) is a curious record of relative failure, in which nothing quite came right, and Bismarck almost seemed to have lost his earlier tactical skill and good judgment (Section E).

The theory that seems best to fit the facts is that he really had, through some degree of misjudgment or over-confidence, failed during the first years of the empire to appreciate the futility of minatory policies unsupported by force. Before 1870 provocative diplomacy had prepared the way for the swift blow, delivered in accordance with his own timing: now he was using only the threat of force to secure his position. The situation could not but strengthen his pessimistic view on German vulnerability. The lesson of the 1875 crisis was the need for less direct and explicit assertions of strength. After all, if the era of wars was over, why not say so? Accordingly there was a marked change of tactics after 1875. Increased emphasis was laid on Germany's desire for peace and absence of expansive aims. Even when acquiring colonies in the eighties he continued to insist that he was no colonial man. Instead, he professed friendship for all powers including, after 1877, France; promised diplomatic support for reasonable expansion and territorial acquisitions on their part (providing Germany was not expected to quarrel with their rivals), and offered himself on suitable occasions as a mediator. This policy was first worked out in the Near Eastern crisis of 1875-8 (Section F). Bismarck was much consulted, sympathetic, ready with proposals, available as 'an honest broker'—and determined not to be involved. From the discussions emerged suggestions for Russo-Austrian division of interests in the Balkans, British concentration on Egypt, and French expansion into north-west Africa. He did not want them to fight, but to be sufficiently involved in their problems and squabbles to leave Germany alone.

It is not easy to say how far the course of European development in the seventies and eighties would have been different if Bismarck had never attained office: and to guard against the mistake of attributing all crises to his initiative we must note that all the specific contemporary European issues except that of Alsace-Lorraine were of longer duration. The calculation of alternatives is difficult to make when the new Germany herself had produced the humbler standing of Austria and

France. Certainly, however, the Turkish question, the Roman problem, the new imperialism, and the growing influence on the European rivalries of United States and Russian expansionism were old or developing issues in which he was interested mainly in order to keep Germany out of trouble. In this rather negative sense it can be said that in the eighties European developments for a time corresponded with his wishes, and no one doubted his towering eminence. Germany's strength became greater in manpower, economic development, and probably military resources after his retirement; but her political authority declined.

His greatest failure was in his relations with Russia. France after 1871 was irreconcilable, but Bismarck had brought about this situation with his eyes open in 1870-1. In the case of Russia on the other hand he was never able after 1871 to marshal arguments and offer tangible inducements sufficient to create the genuine intimacy which he desired. Overall responsibility for this is not easy to define. Before 1870 Bismarck had courted Russia, derived much benefit from her tolerant attitude towards Prussian empire building, and done something to repay the debt (and, it would have seemed, consolidate the relationship) by his support over the Black Sea clauses at the London conference, which completed its sittings on 13 March 1871. On the other hand his support for her Balkan ambitions, as in the agreement of March 1868 (D,4), was and remained circumscribed. Was this ingratitude? From time to time the Russians said so, and Bismarck would reply by hinting (as in October 1876) at a willingness for more far-reaching cooperation than the tsar himself seems to have desired. From the late fifties onward there was always a pro-French element, varying in influence, in Russian court and governmental circles. Alexander II and conservative Russian opinion still felt concern for the European balance and the ordering of European affairs in the Holy Alliance tradition, with continuing uneasiness at Bismarck's flouting of the concert. Gorchakov undoubtedly aspired to a mediatory role in Europe and could play it to Bismarck's disadvantage until forced on the diplomatic defensive by the Near Eastern crisis of 1877-8. These Russo-German tensions, largely personal, were exacerbated by the panslavist furore which mounted after 1875 and led Bismarck to agitated speculation as to the existence of a panslavist revolutionary plot which might engulf the tsar and then Germany. He resembled Napoleon I in his fear of revolution and in his vastly greater assurance in handling the more conventional crises of diplomacy and war. He spoke feelingly in October 1880 of the 'revolutionary quartette on the

G string', Gorchakov, Gambetta, Garibaldi, and Gladstone, as disturbers of the peace.[4]

The alliance system which Bismarck elaborated between 1879 and 1883 was essentially an attempt to establish sufficient control over the minds of Russia's leaders to neutralize anti-German, anti-Austrian, and pro-French gestures; on the Russian side alliance with Germany was similarly accepted as a means of neutralizing German animosity. The seriousness of the crisis period of 1885-8 was basically due to Russian and French impatience with the restrictiveness of the Bismarckian arrangements, which operated automatically to their disadvantage. The elaboration of his highly secret and contradictory devices to ensure peace (which was probably never seriously threatened) ranks with his diplomacy of 1863-6 as a classic of cabinet diplomacy (Section I); but the crisis petered out without any dramatic finale, and with little of tangible satisfaction for him. The Three Emperors' Alliance disappeared in the process. The Russians remained threatening and querulous. His unsuccessful efforts to secure an alliance with Britain or to protect Italy against France in 1889 suggest that Europe was freeing itself from his not unbenevolent grip some time before the young Emperor William II freed himself from his overmighty servant in March 1890.

[4] G. A. Rein, *Die Revolution in der Politik Bismarcks* (Göttingen, 1957), p. 207.

A

PROBLEMS OF PRUSSIAN FOREIGN POLICY: BISMARCK AS DIPLOMAT, 1851-1862

In the Olmütz agreement of 29 November 1850 the Prussian government, headed by the arch-conservative Otto von Manteuffel, agreed to abandon plans for north German unification under Prussia which might have meant war with both Austria and Russia. An Austro-Prussian defensive alliance was signed in 1851. Bismarck defended the unpopular decision with sardonic arguments from expediency in the Prussian Chamber on 3 December 1850 (3), and spoke politely about Austria.

His appointment as Prussian envoy to the revived German *Bund* at Frankfurt was partly a reward for his loyalty. But he had also it would seem been chosen as a resolute man for a difficult job. After taking up his appointment on 11 May 1851 he rapidly familiarized himself (under the tutorship for the first three months of an experienced diplomat, Theodor von Rochow) with the routine of diplomatic business. His famous comment at the end of a week on diplomatic charlatanry must in the circumstances be regarded as an attempt to amuse his young wife rather than as a considered judgment (4).

But during his eight years at Frankfurt he had much to say about every facet of the problem of securing Prussia's rise to dominant power in Germany, and this replaced the defence of aristocratic conservatism as the dominant purpose of his political life. He rapidly became convinced of the impossibility of sharing power with Austria, who sought after Olmütz to maintain her predominance more ostentatiously than she had done before 1848. Bismarck's task, as he saw it, was to thwart the tricks and pretensions of Austrian representatives, while at the same time inducing the lesser German states to follow the Prussian lead whenever possible.

This energetic assertiveness was not altogether what the Prussian government wanted, and Bismarck could not persuade either the king, Frederick William IV, or Manteuffel to run the risk of an open quarrel with Austria. Nor is it likely that he desired anything more during his first years at Frankfurt than to establish respect for his own formidable and rancorous personality and to leave Prussia free to use or defy Austria as she saw fit. A number of lines of argument, some difficult to reconcile with each other, run through his masterly correspondence with Manteuffel and with Leopold von Gerlach, the king's confidant. His own views as to the possibilities of the international situation varied from time to time, and he was adroit in adapting his arguments to the viewpoint of his correspondents.

But in terms of foreign policy he desired the dominance of Germany by Prussia and at this period he believed that Austria must be forced to acquiesce in this by political manoeuvring on Prussia's part rather than by force. He accepted the view that Prussia was not strong enough to fight at this stage, and he knew that in any case the will to do so was lacking. He soon rejected, if he had ever seriously held it, the hope that Austria would concede leadership or profitable terms of partnership to Prussia without a struggle. And he did not think that in any case Austria was of much value to Prussia as leader or ally (5). The alternative courses were to immobilize Austria inside the Confederation by turning the votes of a majority of the smaller states against her, or to rely on foreign, and particularly French and Russian, aid.

From the beginning of 1853 he urged the desirability of keeping the way open for alliance with France. During the Crimean war, when Austria managed to displease both sides by opposing Russia diplomatically without fighting her, Bismarck entertained bold plans for forcing Prussia's terms on Austria as the price of support, with an alliance with Russia (which he preferred) or the western powers, should Austria refuse. Frederick William, however, renewed the Austro-Prussian defensive alliance in April 1854, and could not forget the tradition of family loyalty to the Habsburgs, although his brother and heir, Prince William, inclined to the western powers. In the end, Prussia did nothing decisive or compromising during the war, and Bismarck was left to renew his arguments when it was over.

He had shrewdly anticipated that France and Russia would draw together after the peace of Paris (30 March 1856), and that in some circumstances England and Austria might draw together in opposition. He now renewed his arguments for the utilization of foreign alliances for Prussia's aggrandizement, without finally excluding the possibility of cooperation with a more accommodating Austrian regime. He found it necessary to explain to von Gerlach that his policy was one of sheer expediency, and that he would be equally satisfied to see Prussian troops fire on any foreign army if it suited Prussian policy; in times of peace, it was wasteful either to quarrel with or offer favours to foreign countries without a specific advantage in return (6). This stark realism was a little too intellectualized for the Prussian conservatives, who equated Bonapartism with revolution, and looked to Russia for comfort, while apprehensive of both Russian and French 'Caesarism'. When Bismarck, in a long memorial to Manteuffel of 18 May 1857, argued in favour of closer relations with France (7), Gerlach objected that Prussia could be no more than a 'humble third' in an alliance with France and Russia. Bismarck proposed to find the answer to this objection partly in skilful balancing between the Franco-Russian and Anglo-Austrian groups, partly in the strengthening of

Prussia by army reform and by harnessing German nationalism. This idea appears in his memorial of 18 May 1857 and was elaborated in an even lengthier document of March 1858, known as the 'Booklet' (8). Without being sentimentally affected by the idea of German nationalism he argued that self-interest and the moral force of the nationalist idea could be used to secure the acquiescence of the smaller German states in Prussia's plans. In another document, the Baden-Baden memorial of October 1861, he explored the possibility of introducing as part of a revised Zollverein, a 'Zollparlament' which would have obvious political uses (10).

This opportunist use of German nationalism had a double significance in connexion with the 'grossdeutsch-kleindeutsch' controversy. These terms referred to the two principal political attitudes of 1848, and became familiar after the founding of the 'Deutscher Nationalverein' (German National Union) in September 1859. Although looking on the whole to Prussia to lead a united Germany (the 'kleindeutsch' solution) its members hoped for some satisfactory accommodation with Austria. Bismarck's inclination was always to justify Prussia's leadership on grounds of natural efficiency (a 'seaworthy frigate') and he was sceptical about the reality of nationalistic sentiment; he had even talked in 1848 about the 'German swindle'. Nevertheless, he and other Prussian propagandists were alive to the need to discredit Austria's leadership qualifications. It could be argued that she was a middle-European rather than a truly German state, and that Viennese policy since the days of Metternich was conceived far more on middle-European than on German lines.[1]

Frederick William was incapacitated by a stroke in October 1857, Prince William became regent, and king in January 1861. Bismarck's revolutionary plans for utilizing German nationalism in the Prussian cause did not at first convince Prince William, who in 1858 preferred friendship with Austria and England and a mildly liberal political orientation. Manteuffel was dismissed and Bismarck was removed from Frankfurt to St. Petersburg, where he took up the embassy in April 1859 (9). His hopes of securing government office fluctuated during the next few years; he was recalled from Russia in March 1862 but was then sent as ambassador to Paris, where he did something to encourage Napoleon III's belief that Prussia might prove a useful and accommodating ally of France.

1   Adolescent Dilemmas

I left school at Easter 1832, a normal product of our state system of education; a Pantheist, and, if not a Republican, at least with the persuasion that the Republic was the most rational form of govern-

---

[1] Cf Gerhard Ritter, *Lebendige Vergangenheit* (Munich, 1958), chapter on 'Grossdeutsch und Kleindeutsch in 19 Jahrhundert', pp. 109, 114; Otto Becker, *Bismarcks Ringen um Deutschlands Gestaltung* (Heidelberg, 1958), p. 76.

ment; reflecting too upon the causes which could decide millions of men permanently to obey *one man*, when all the while I was hearing from grown up people much bitter or contemptuous criticism of their rulers. . . . These impressions remained in the stage of theoretical reflections, and were not strong enough to extirpate my innate Prussian monarchical sentiments. My historical sympathies remained on the side of authority. . . . Every German prince who resisted the Emperor before the Thirty Years' war roused my ire; but from the Great Elector onwards I was partisan enough to take an anti-imperial view, and to find it natural that things should have been in readiness for the Seven Years' war. Yet the German-National feeling remained so strong in me that, at the beginning of my University life, I at once entered into relations with the *Burschenschaft*, or group of students which made the promotion of a national sentiment its aim. . . . In my first half-year at Göttingen occurred the Hambach festival (May 27, 1832), the 'festal ode' of which still remains in my memory; in my third the Frankfort outbreak (April 3, 1833). These manifestations revolted me. Mob interference with political authority conflicted with my Prussian schooling, and I returned to Berlin with less Liberal opinions than when I quitted it; but this reaction was again somewhat mitigated when I was brought into immediate connexion with the workings of the political machine. Upon foreign politics, with which the public at that time occupied itself but little, my views, as regards the War of Liberation, were taken from the standpoint of a Prussian officer. On looking at the map, the possession of Strasburg by France exasperated me, and a visit to Heidelberg, Spires and the Palatinate made me feel revengeful and militant. . . .

R & R, i, 1-3

2 The Prussian as Diplomat

So far as, at my then age, I seriously thought at all of an official career, I had diplomacy in view, even after my application to the minister Ancillon had evoked very little encouragement thereto from him. . . . The minister had the impression that the category of our 'home-made' Prussian squirarchy did not furnish him with the desirable material to draw upon for our diplomacy, and was not adapted to make up for the want of address which he found in the *personnel* of this branch of the service. This impression was not absolutely unjustified. As minister, I have always had a fellow-provincial's kindness for native-born

Prussian diplomatists, but my official sense of duty has rarely allowed me to gratify this preference; as a rule only when the personages in question were transferred to a diplomatic from a military position. In purely Prussian civil-diplomats, who have never, or only inadequately, come under the influence of military discipline, I have as a rule observed too strong a tendency to criticism, to 'cocksureness', to opposition and personal touchiness, intensified by the discontent which the Old Prussian gentleman's feeling of equality experiences when a man of his own rank is put over his head, or becomes his superior otherwise than under military conditions.... An acquaintance with languages (after the fashion in which it is possessed even by head-waiters) was with us readily made the basis for a belief in diplomacy as one's vocation, especially so long as our Ambassadorial reports, particularly those *ad regem*, had to be in French; as was the official rule in force (though not always followed), till I became minister....

R & R, i, 3-5

3 Bismarck opposes War: 3 December 1850

Speech at sitting of the Second Chamber of the Prussian Landtag following the signature of the Olmütz agreement

... what kind of a war is this? Not an expedition of isolated regiments to Schleswig or Baden, not a military promenade through troubled provinces, but a major war against two of the three great continental powers,[2] whilst the third mobilizes on our frontier, eager for conquest and well aware that in Cologne there is treasure to be found which could end the French Revolution and give their rulers the French Imperial crown. A war, gentlemen, which will begin by forcing us to give up some of the remoter Prussian provinces, in which a large part of Prussia will be inundated by enemy forces, and which will bring to our provinces the full horrors of war. A war, it can be assumed, that the Minister of Public Worship, who has jurisdiction over the servants of religion, peace and love, must loathe to the bottom of his heart. (Laughter.) A war, which the Minister for Trade and Industry must be convinced will begin by destroying the public welfare entrusted to his care, and which the Finance Minister can only desire when the money can no longer be left in the royal coffers. And yet I would not shrink from such a war, indeed I would advise it, if someone could prove to me that it was necessary, or show me a worthy goal which could only

[2] Note in original: Austria and Russia.

be attained by it and in no other way. Why do large states go to war nowadays? The only sound basis for a large state, and this is what distinguishes it from a small state, is state egoism and not romanticism, and it is not worthy of a great state to fight for something that is not in its own interest. Show me therefore, Gentlemen, an objective worthy of war, and I will agree with you. It is easy for a statesman, whether in the Cabinet or the Chamber, to use the public wind to blow the trumpets of war, and to sit at home by his own fireside or make thundering speeches from the rostrum, and leave it to the musketeer, pouring out his life's blood on the snowy wastes, to decide whether the system will bring glory or victory or no. Nothing is easier, but woe unto the statesman who at this time does not seek a cause for the war that will endure when the war is over. . . .

GW, x, 102-4

4 An early Judgment on Diplomacy

Bismarck to his wife, 18 May 1851

. . . In the art of using many words to say nothing at all I am making rapid progress, I write reports of many pages which read neatly and clearly like newspaper leaders, and if Manteuffel, when he has read them, can say what is in them, he is cleverer than I am. Each of us behaves as though he thinks the others are brimming over with thoughts and plans, if he could only formulate them, and yet all of us together are not a whit wiser as to what will or should become of Germany, than Dutken Sauer.[3] No one, not even the most malevolent sceptic of a democrat, would believe what charlatanry and pomposity there is in this diplomacy. . . .

GW, xiv(i), 213

5 Prussia a Trim and Sea-worthy Frigate

Bismarck to Manteuffel, private letter, 15 February 1854

. . . I cannot deny that I have been somewhat alarmed to learn from friends' letters that in His Majesty's entourage there is a kind of gloom at the thought of the isolation we should find ourselves in after a breach with Russia, and a feeling that it is essential to seek a closer tie with Austria and avoid all disputes with her. I should be very uneasy

[3] Apparently a local allusion. Another version gives 'Dutken Sommer'.

if we sought refuge from a possible storm by hitching our trim and sea-worthy frigate to that worm-eaten old Austrian man-of-war. Of the two we are the better swimmers and a welcome ally for *anyone*; if we want to give up our possible isolation and strict neutrality it would be difficult just now to avoid the appearance of anxiously seeking for support, whereas later we could lay down conditions in return for our aid. Great crises produce the weather conditions which promote the growth of Prussia, and we have used them fearlessly, even ruthlessly. If we want to make further growth, then at least we must not be afraid to stand alone with [our] 400,000 men, particularly while the other powers are fighting each other and thus we, by taking sides with each of them, can make a better bargain than by an early and unconditional alliance with such an ineffective fighter and insincere partner as Austria.

GW i, 427

6 Bismarck disclaims Partiality for Foreign Powers

Bismarck to Leopold von Gerlach, 11 May 1857

My dear Friend,

... If you want to send your family there, it is high time to seek a habitation, and to let me know what you will need; I will then arrange for it with pleasure. I understand from Berlin that I am looked on at court as a Bonapartist. But in this they do me an injustice. In the year '50 I was accused by our opponents of a treacherous penchant for Austria, and we were called the Berlin Viennese; later on they decided that we smelt of Russia leather and called us the Spree-Cossacks. At that time if I was questioned as to whether I was a Russian or a Westerner, I always answered that I was a Prussian, and that my ideal in foreign policy was freedom from all prejudice, and that all decisions should be independent of any appearance of hostility towards, or partiality for, foreign powers and their rulers. As regards other countries, in my life so far I have felt myself to be in sympathy only with England and its inhabitants, and from time to time still feel this; but the people don't want us to love them, and if anyone were to prove to me that it would be in the best interests of a healthy and well-thought-out policy, I would have equal satisfaction in seeing our troops fire on French, Russian, English or Austrian troops. In times of peace

I consider it to be a wanton waste of one's resources to attract or foster ill-feeling, unless it is combined with a practical political aim, and to sacrifice the freedom to make future decisions to vague and unreciprocated sympathies, and to make the kind of concessions that Austria expects of us at the moment concerning Rastatt, merely out of kindness of heart and 'love of approbation'.[4] If we cannot expect any compensation for such a kind act, then we should withold our concession too, as we might have the opportunity later to use it as a *quid pro quo*. Usefulness for the Confederation should not be the exclusive guideline for Prussian policy, for the most useful thing for the Bund would be, without any doubt at all, to subordinate ourselves and all the German governments, militarily, politically and commercially, under Austria in the Zollverein; under united leadership the Bund could achieve other things in peace and war, and would be in a strong defensive position in case of war. I only mention this, in order to show that the consolidation of Austria's military position in South Germany cannot be a matter of complete indifference, even if it is advantageous to the Bund, particularly from Austria's point of view.

Briefwechsel des Generals Leopold von Gerlach mit ... Otto von Bismarck (Berlin, 1893), pp. 335-6

7   The Case for a French Alliance

Bismarck's Memorial for Manteuffel, 18 May 1857

... The best compromise would be to cultivate relations between France and Prussia. France could side with Austria or the Rhine states, and could easily win the support of both; but French interests are opposed to an alliance with Austria, and one with the central states would alienate Prussia, and Prussia is the more powerful element in Germany and a state with a future. The friendship of Prussia opens up to France the prospect of considerable advantages. It offers her a non-English continental prop, and as such will have the effect of making English policy more considerate towards France and less likely to incur a breach with her without careful thought; yet it will not seem like a challenge to England, as an alliance with Russia would; it will form a link which will keep open for France the chance of a Russian alliance in case of need, and give her a better hold on the conditions for it; it

[4] In English in the original.

will relieve France of the necessity, or the temptation, of securing an alliance with Russia prematurely or precipitately, and thereby bringing about a breach with England; at the same time it holds out the prospect of an alliance which will undoubtedly dominate the continent, as soon as it is completed by the inclusion of Russia, and it will have a moderating effect on England. These advantages make it obvious that France sets great store on closer relations with us, or, if we do not want that, on at least the semblance of closer relations. For Prussia the gain will be in the form of delaying tactics in Germany; for while France is more concerned about our goodwill than that of the middle states, the latter will lose the chance of a Rheinbund, and they will have to turn to us, as with Austria alone they will not feel safe and protected, as long as that country has no alliance with Russia.

The fostering of friendly relations with France need not therefore have any adverse effect on the peace of Europe; on the contrary, it would be an increased guarantee for peace. It would lessen the likelihood of a breach between England and France, it would postpone the possibility of a Franco-Russian alliance for war purposes, and would give us, if it should come to that, the chance to have a moderating influence on its form and aims, and would provide it with such a superior force, that it is unlikely that a continental war would be waged against it; furthermore it would be the means, and perhaps the sole means, of preserving the form and entity of the German Bund as a basis on which to build, and of affording ourselves a decisive influence on it. Even the outward appearance of close relations between Prussia and France will have a powerful influence in this sense; the Emperor Napoleon, for his part, openly admits the interest which he has in fostering this impression, and he would, if we showed any signs of rapprochement, himself make a more definite gesture to that end. . . .

GW, ii, 218-22

8 Extracts from 'the Booklet'

[Bismarck's memorandum of late March 1858 for Prince William was entitled 'Some observations on Prussia's attitude to the Bund'. It was known as 'Das kleine Buch des Herrn v. Bismarck' (i.e. the Booklet) because of its length.]

. . . But a nearer danger is that Prussia will have a formal disagreement with the Bund, in that the majority will make resolutions which Prussia cannot agree to without injury to her independence. The most accommodating attitude to the Bund has its limits, and in negotiations with Austria any concession leads to new demands. If things go on as they have recently . . . the time is not far off when Prussia will accuse the majority of exceeding their powers, and the majority accuse Prussia of opposing Bund resolutions, both therefore guilt of a breach of the Bund.

To put Prussia in this position is perhaps the aim of her opponents' policy; how and when such a situation can be exploited by them in the near future depends on the constellation of European politics, according to whether they seem to favour a more or less bold confrontation of Prussia. . . .

(*Prussia's remedy*.) The position of Prussia would perhaps be better if the Bund did not exist; the closer relations with neighbours which Prussia needs would have been brought about, and under Prussia's leadership. But seeing that it does exist, and the misuse of its institutions against Prussia has some prospect of success, Prussia's task can only be to fulfil faithfully all its indubitable obligations to the Bund in peace and war, but to curtail at the expense of the independence of the various members any development of the power of the Bund which goes beyond the strict letter of the treaty. By doing this Prussia would not be in any way unfaithful to her German ideals, she would only be resisting the pressure of a conception, invented by her opponents, that 'Bundestag' and 'Deutschland' are identical, and that Prussia's German-mindedness should be judged according to the extent of her submission to the majority of the Bund members. No state has the urge and opportunity to assert its German point of view independently of the Bund assembly to the same extent as Prussia, and it may at the same time prove that Prussia is of more importance to the middle and smaller states than a majority of nine votes for Prussia.

Prussian interests coincide exactly with those of most of the Bund *countries* except Austria, but not with those of the Bund *governments*, and there is nothing more German than the development of Prussia's particular interests, properly understood. . . .

GW, ii, 316-17

9   Bismarck in St. Petersburg, 1862

[Friedrich von Holstein arrives in St. Petersburg in January 1861 as an attaché.]

. . . when I presented myself, he held out his hand and said, 'You are welcome.' As he stood there, tall, erect, unsmiling, I saw him as he was later to appear to his family and the rest of the world: 'A man who allows no one to know him intimately.' . . .

At that time Bismarck was forty-five, slightly bald, with fair hair turning grey; not noticeably corpulent; sallow complexion. Never gay, even when telling amusing anecdotes, a thing he did only occasionally, in particularly congenial company. Total impression one of a dissatisfied man, partly a hypochondriac, partly a man insufficiently reconciled to the quiet life led in those days by the Prussian representative in St. Petersburg. His every utterance revealed that for him action and existence were one and the same thing. 'The 1848 revolution must have been a harassing time for you,' I once said to him. 'There was so much to do that there was no time to feel harassed,' was the reply. . . . The main attraction of [the] Frankfurt period for him had been the fact that it was one of constant strife. . . .

The Holstein Memoirs (Cambridge, 1955), ed. N. Rich and M. H. Fisher, pp. 4, 5

10 Bismarck's Baden-Baden Memorial, July-October 1861

. . . In order to proceed towards [a durable union], a national representation of the German people in the central government is perhaps the only unifying force which can provide a sufficient counterpoise to the tendency of the individual dynasties to follow divergent policies. . . . The form and extent of such a representation can only be determined by very careful consideration, and by agreement between the Bund states. It could not go beyond decisions about the military force of the Bund, customs and commercial legislation, and the field of allied material interests, leaving the governmental authority within each state unimpaired. Some guarantee of the intelligence and conservative attitude of the representatives would be provided if they were not chosen directly by the population, but by the various Landtage. . . . The practical realization of a German national representation has so far not been possible by federal constitutional means, and could only go hand in hand with a complete overhaul of the central government. But it might be a less hopeless task to set up other national arrangements in the same way that the Zollverein was created.

Whether and how the Zollverein can be renewed after completion of its present term, only time can decide. It is, however, desirable that it should not continue in its present form, under which the right of veto of the various members can hinder the development of our commercial legislation. Here, too, besides introducing the right to pass resolutions on at least a two-thirds majority, further difficulties could most easily be solved by committees of varying numbers from the Estate assemblies of the various states, who by consulting together would try and settle the differences of opinion amongst the governments. Such a 'Zollparlament' could, under certain circumstances and with skilful leadership, pave the way for agreements in other spheres into which German states would more likely be prepared to enter if they always remained terminable on the giving of notice. . . .

GW, iii, 266-70

B

THE FIRST IMPACT, 1862-1864

Bismarck's appointment as minister president and foreign minister of Prussia on 22 September 1862 was made at a point of crisis in both the domestic and foreign affairs of Prussia. But he abounded in self-confidence, or at least in the determination to show it (2). The promise of unqualified support of King William's action in defying the parliamentary majority made it difficult for him to press the king for concessions over the problem of military reorganization, although this is what he would have preferred in view of the foreign situation. Unknown to the king he did make some efforts to patch up a compromise settlement, but the king was confirmed in his stubborn refusal to give way by the die-hard members of his 'military cabinet'. So by the beginning of 1863 Bismarck had settled down to rule Prussia without a properly voted budget, relying on the crown's residual powers under the constitution.

Bismarck's first major speech in his new office was made on 30 September 1862 to the budget committee of the lower chamber of the Landtag. While he was bound to try to turn the minds of the deputies away from the domestic deadlock he no doubt meant what he said about the urgency of the foreign problem. Speaking in witty, striking, agitated, and at times threatening tones, he talked about the primacy of blood and iron; the speech seemed provocative and ill-timed even to his friends (3). It indicates nevertheless his understanding that only a successful foreign policy could ensure Prussia's political future and his own.

During the next two years three problems, distinct in origin but each dependent on his fluctuating relations with the governments of Austria, Russia, France, and England, matured his diplomatic technique without finally establishing his political dominance in Europe.

(a) *Austria and the Bund.* When Bismarck came to office a severe struggle with Austria was at its height over Austrian plans to strengthen the *Bund* at Prussia's expense and Prussia's plans to reform the Zollverein (the north German customs union), ultimately to Austria's disadvantage. In December 1861 Prussia had vetoed a Saxon plan for a tripartite organization of the Confederation by arguing that only a north German federation led by Prussia could satisfy German needs. Austria had countered this move by plans for a strengthened Confederation which if accepted by the lesser German states would have reinforced Austrian leadership, inevitably at Prussia's expense. In spite of violent Prussian objections, five of the middle German states supported Austria in August 1862 and the plan was sent forward for elaboration in committee.

The Zollverein, economically advantageous to the small German states and dominated by Prussia, had been formed in 1834 and renewed in 1853 with the continued exclusion of Austria, but with a promise to consider her case for entry when the existing treaties expired at the end of 1865. A Franco-Prussian free trade treaty of March 1862 would, however, if approved by the other German members of the Zollverein, make Austria's entry impossible, for her economy was ill-equipped to stand up to the rigours of competition in a great free-trade zone. In spite of anguished Austrian protests Prussia took steps in August 1862 to complete the new Zollverein arrangements.

Thus Bismarck, on his entry into office, had merely to continue, although more forcefully, a ready-made challenge to Austrian pretensions. Talking to Bismarck in June 1862, the Emperor Napoleon had shown interest in a Franco-Prussian alliance, and although King William shied away from this idea he counted, as did Bismarck, on benevolent French neutrality. To the alarm of Count Rechberg, Austrian foreign minister since 1859, Bismarck talked openly of the possibility of an Austro-Prussian war. At the same time he frightened many of the smaller German states with warnings of wrath to come in the event of a Prussian defeat on the constitutional issue.

However, in December 1862 Napoleon let it be known that he had no intention of giving Prussia carte blanche, and Bismarck found it expedient to keep alive the possibility of Austro-Prussian cooperation. The war danger receded for the time being when the Austrian proposal was narrowly defeated on 22 January. An Austrian attempt to revive it in the autumn of 1863 was defeated only when Bismarck managed to persuade King William to ignore a personal approach from the Emperor Francis Joseph.

(b) *The Polish Insurrection.* Bismarck's hopes of France were further reduced by Napoleon's reaction to the Alvensleben convention of 8 February 1863. The Polish insurrection against Russian conscription measures broke out on 21 January. As a precautionary measure the Prussian government at once sent large forces into Prussian Poland, and despatched General Gustav von Alvensleben, one of the two or three most trusted of King William's inner ring of military advisers, to discuss common measures with the Russians. Prince Gorchakov, to whom the insurrection had come as an unfortunate interruption of a more Liberal policy towards the Poles, did not need or want help. He had to agree to the convention (which was drafted in the Russian foreign office) because the tsar, Alexander II, did not wish to offend his uncle, King William. The convention provided for cooperation in rounding up insurgents on either side of the frontier (4,i), and was immediately accepted by Prussia (4,ii).

In his memoirs Bismarck admits that the convention was not demanded by the military situation, but claims that it was a diplomatic success because the tsar's decision meant the defeat of the liberal tendencies represented by the philo-Polish party led by Gorchakov. In reality the tsar's reactions are better represented by a private comment on 22 February: 'One must admit that our dear Bismarck is a terrible blunderer.'[1] The appearance of concerted action against the Poles led to a wave of pro-Polish sentiment in France and England, and Napoleon, who did not wish to quarrel with Russia if he could help it, promptly invited the British and Austrian governments to join him in remonstrating in Berlin. Reports of joint talks between Britain, France, and Austria conjured up the spectre of the Crimean coalition. The British and Austrians refused the French invitation, but the French and British envoys spoke bluntly in Berlin (5).

Bismarck was believed to have offered his resignation, perhaps on 23 February. Anyway, he let it be known before the end of February that the convention was unlikely to come into force, and Gorchakov quickly concurred. Soon the British government was pointing out that the main offender against the Poles was after all Russia. Bismarck from this point maintained his more reserved attitude, and the later stages of the Polish crisis were essentially Russia's problem.

(c) *The Problem of the Duchies.* The alignment of the powers, Bismarck's injudicious Polish activity notwithstanding, was moving to Prussia's advantage during 1863. By taking the lead in pressure on Russia in the interest of the Poles, Napoleon had destroyed the last hopes of a Franco-Russian alliance, without consolidating his ties with London or Vienna. In both capitals his general restlessness and his ambitions in the Rhineland aroused fears, which the tsar shared, for the integrity of Germany. A suggestion by Bismarck to the Russian ambassador, Baron Paul d'Oubril, on 3 September 1863 of a Prussian-Russian-British alignment reflected his anti-Austrian rather than anti-French inclinations at the moment. But the Russians, who were shocked by the fierceness of the Austro-Prussian quarrel over the constitutional question in August, had no intention of encouraging Prussia to fight Austria, with the consequent destruction of the anti-French barrier. Nevertheless, Bismarck's emphatic appeals for Russian support drew sympathetic assurances from the Russians (8), with some Russian pressure on Austria to modify her political demands on Prussia over the Confederation. Looking round rather desperately for a friend, Napoleon renewed his soundings in Berlin, and made a proposal, which was generally distrusted, for a congress to solve outstanding issues. Britain completed the ruin of the Anglo-French rapprochement by rejecting the congress proposal in November. And by this point Austria, isolated and depressed, had decided that it would be wiser for a time to collaborate with Prussia.

Thus when the crisis over the Danish duchies of Schleswig, Holstein, and Lauenburg became acute in December 1863 there was little inclination in any capital to seek a quarrel with Prussia over the issues. Six states—Austria, Britain, France, Russia, Prussia, and Sweden, but not the other members of the German Confederation—had signed the London treaty of 8 May 1852, which provided for the ultimate succession of Prince Charles of Glucksburg and left

[1] *R & R*, i, 342-3; W. E. Mosse, *op. cit.*, p. 115.

the three duchies in the enjoyment of their existing privileges under Danish rule (1). On 30 March 1963 King Frederick VII had proclaimed a new constitution by which Schleswig became merely a Danish province; Holstein retained a partly independent position, but on financial terms considered unduly favourable to the state as a whole. Holstein was predominantly German, and a member of the German Confederation; Danes were more numerous in Schleswig, but the German population there was growing. Danish public opinion was so fiercely nationalist that when Frederick died his successor, Charles IX, felt he had no alternative but to ratify the new constitution on 18 November 1863.

Bismarck's early moves were aimed at accustoming the other powers to accept the Austro-Prussian initiative as the most reasonable way of handling Denmark's quarrel with the Confederation. He confided to the Prussian Crown Council on 4 February 1864 his intention to annex the duchies in due course, but he continued to tell the world that he preferred a return to the treaty of 8 May 1852, as he and Austria had announced on 28 November 1863. The Austro-Prussian attitude commended itself to the other powers because the alternative, urged by the liberal-nationalist elements in the Confederation in a great rally in Frankfurt on 21 December 1863, was the setting-up of an independent state of Schleswig-Holstein under the Duke of Augustenburg, a solution wildly popular even in Prussia. Bismarck disliked this plan because it conflicted with his basic aim and because the small state would lean to Austria; Austria disliked it because she thought that the state would be dominated by Prussia. Furthermore he was determined, as he told von der Goltz in his letter of reprimand of 24 December, that Prussia should assert her independent position as a great power and not merely drift along as a member of the *Bund* (7). As Christian could not give way the Confederation proceeded to a 'Federal Execution' which meant that on 24 December Saxon and Hanoverian troops entered Holstein, with Austrian and Prussian forces in the rear.

Bismarck had no difficulty in representing himself as a moderating influence, striving to bring both the German Confederation and the Danish king back to the 1852 position (9). In conversation with Napoleon's envoy, Count Fleury, he showed interest on 24 December in the idea of a congress in Paris on the question, and he revealed no hostility towards French aspirations in the Rhineland (8). French and British uneasiness at the invasion of Denmark did not in the circumstances overcome their reluctance to aid Denmark by force, and the Austro-Prussian forces proceeded to occupy Schleswig; the divisions on this point among the smaller German states prevented them from sharing the risks or the glory of this advance. There was further French and British talk of intervention as the German troops advanced; but nothing effective was done before the Prussians captured the last Danish stronghold at Düppel on 18 April.

When a conference met in London on 25 April on Britain's invitation Austria agreed with Prussia in announcing that a return to the 1852 position was impossible. The possibility of a Prussian annexation was now looming unpleasantly before the powers. Bismarck had already broached this idea to

Rechberg, holding out the prospect of compensation and Prussian friendship in exchange. He had not publicly ruled out the idea of a personal union under King Christian, who however showed no interest in it. To stave off annexation, Austria now rather desperately chose the Augustenburg plan; Bismarck, while supporting it before the conference at the end of May, was not nonplussed, for he had already drawn up onerous conditions which would make the state a dependency of Prussia (10). King Christian eased Bismarck's course by refusing all compromise, and the war was resumed on 28 June. France would not intervene, and not surprisingly failed to persuade Britain to do so (11). Denmark, speedily defeated, soon gave in completely. In the treaty of Vienna of 30 October 1864 the King of Denmark ceded his rights in the three duchies completely to Austria and Prussia.

Bismarck had triumphed, in a confused and complicated situation, because his aims were clear to himself while others were undecided, and because he showed unfailing judgment as to the limits of successful action and persuasion in each phase of the game. His reputation was growing, but was underrated by many who still saw only a headstrong politician among diffident neighbours.

1   Treaty of London, 8 May 1852

IN THE NAME OF THE MOST HOLY AND INDIVISIBLE TRINITY
Balance of Power in Europe

[The rulers of Austria, the United Kingdom, France, Prussia, Russia, and Norway and Sweden] taking into consideration that the maintenance of the Integrity of the Danish Monarchy, as connected with the general interests of the Balance of Power in Europe is of high importance to the preservation of Peace, and that an Arrangement by which the Succession to the whole of the Dominions now united under the sceptre of His Majesty the King of Denmark should devolve upon the male line, to the exclusion of females, would be the best means of securing the Integrity of that Monarchy, have resolved, at the invitation of His Danish Majesty, to conclude a Treaty, in order to give to the arrangements relating to such order of Succession an additional pledge of stability by an act of European acknowledgment. . . .

Article I. After having taken into serious consideration the interests of his Monarchy, His Majesty the King of Denmark, with the assent of His Royal Highness the Hereditary Prince, and of his nearest cognates, entitled to the Succession by the Royal Law of Denmark, as well as in concert with His Majesty the Emperor of All the Russias, Head of the elder Branch of the House of Holstein-Gottorp, having declared his wish to regulate the order of Succession in his dominions in such manner that, in default of issue male in a direct line from King Frederick III of Denmark, his Crown should devolve upon His Highness the Prince Christian of Schleswig-Holstein-Sonderbourg-Glücksbourg, and upon the issue of the marriage of that Prince with Her Highness the Princess Louisa of Schleswig-Holstein-Sonderbourg-Glücksbourg, born a Princess of Hesse, by order of Primogeniture from Male to Male; the High Contracting Parties, appreciating the wisdom of the views which have determined the eventual adoption of that arrangement, engage by common consent, in case the contemplated contingency should be realized, to acknowledge in His Highness the Prince Christian of Schleswig-Holstein-Sonderbourg-Glücksbourg, and his issue male in the direct line by his marriage with the said Princess, the Right of Succeeding to the whole of the Dominions now united under the sceptre of His Majesty the King of Denmark.

Article II. The High Contracting Parties, acknowledging as permanent the principle of the Integrity of the Danish Monarchy, engage to take into consideration the further propositions which His Majesty the King of Denmark may deem it expedient to address to them in case (which God forbid) the extinction of the issue male, in the direct line, of His Highness the Prince Christian of Schleswig-Holstein-Sonderbourg-Glücksbourg, by his marriage with Her Highness the Princess Louisa of Schleswig-Holstein-Sonderbourg-Glücksbourg, born a Princess of Hesse, should become imminent.

Article III. It is expressly understood that the reciprocal Rights and Obligations of His Majesty the King of Denmark, and of the Germanic Confederation, concerning the Duchies of Holstein and Lauenburg, Rights and Obligations established by the Federal Act of 1815, and by the existing Federal Right, shall not be affected by the present Treaty.

Article IV. The High Contracting Parties reserve to themselves to bring the present Treaty to the knowledge of the other Powers, and to invite them to accede to it. . . .[2]

Hertslet, ii, 1151-5

[2] The powers which did accede were Belgium, Hanover, Hesse-Cassel, Naples, Netherlands, Oldenburg (with reservations), Portugal, Sardinia, Saxony (with reservations), Spain, Tuscany, Württemberg. The following states refused to accede until the views of the German Diet on the subject were made known: Baden, Bavaria, Hesse-Darmstadt, Mecklenburg-Schwerin, Mecklenburg-Strelitz, Saxe-Weimar.

2   Bismarck Prophesies to Disraeli

[During the International Exhibition of 1862 in London the] Russian Ambassador, Baron Brunnow, gave a large dinner . . . at which I was present. Among the guests was the Prussian Minister in Paris, Herr von Bismarck-Schönhausen, who had a long conversation with Disraeli after dinner. The following is part of this conversation which the leader of the Opposition repeated to me on the same evening.

'I shall soon', said in effect the Prussian statesman, 'be compelled to undertake the conduct of the Prussian Government. My first care will be to reorganize the army, with or without the help of the Landtag. The King was right in undertaking this task, but he cannot accomplish it with his present advisers. As soon as the army shall have been brought into such a condition as to inspire respect, I shall seize the first best pretext to declare war against Austria, dissolve the German Diet, subdue the minor States, and give national unity to Germany under Prussian leadership. I have come to say this to the Queen's Ministers.'

Disraeli's commentary on this programme, which has since been carried out step by step, was, 'Take care of that man! He means what he says. . . .'

> Count Vitzthum von Eckstædt,
> *St. Petersburg and London in the*
> *Years 1852–1864* (London, 1887),
> ii, 172

3   'Blood and Iron'

Bismarck's speech on 29 September 1862 to the budget commission of the Prussian Landtag

. . . [He said] he would gladly agree to the budget for 1862, but without giving any prejudicial explanation. A misuse of constitutional powers could happen on any side, and would lead to a reaction from the other side. The crown, for example, could dissolve [parliament] a dozen times, and that would certainly be in accordance with the letter of the Constitution, but it would be a misuse. In the same way it can challenge the budget cancellations as much as it likes: but the limit is difficult to set; shall it be at 6 million, or 16 million, or 60 million?— There are members of the National Union, a party respected because

of the justice of its demands, highly esteemed members, who considered all standing armies superfluous. Now what if a national assembly
were of this opinion! Wouldn't the government have to reject it?—
People speak of the 'sobriety' of the Prussian people. Certainly the
great independence of the individual makes it difficult in Prussia to rule
with the constitution; in France it is different, the independence of the
individual is lacking there. A constitutional crisis is not shameful, but
honourable. Furthermore we are perhaps too 'educated' to put up
with a constitution; we are too critical; the ability to judge government measures and bills of the National Assembly is too widespread;
there are in the country too many subversive elements who have an
interest in revolutionary change. This may sound paradoxical, but it
goes to show how difficult it is in Prussia to carry on a constitutional
existence. . . . We are too ardent, we like to carry too heavy a weight
of armour for our fragile bodies: but we should also make use of it.
Germany doesn't look to Prussia's liberalism, but to its power:
Bavaria, Württemberg, Baden can indulge in liberalism, but no one
will expect them to undertake Prussia's role; Prussia must gather and
consolidate her strength in readiness for the favourable moment, which
has already been missed several times; Prussia's boundaries according
to the Vienna treaties are not favourable to a healthy political life; not
by means of speeches and majority verdicts will the great decisions of
the time be made—that was the great mistake of 1848 and 1849—but
by iron and blood. . . .

GW, x, 140-41

4 The Alvensleben Convention, February 1863

(i) *General von Alvensleben (St. Petersburg) to King William I, 6 February
1863*

Does Your Majesty approve of the text and form of the two following
documents and have I your authorization to sign them? I humbly beg
Your Majesty to let me have your instructions as soon as possible.
Prince Gorchakov would prefer that the secret article, in view of its
political character, should not be included in the treaty but should remain as a secret article. But if Your Majesty should insist on it, then
Prince Gorchakov will yield to Your wishes.

The two courts of Russia and Prussia, recognizing that the events
which have unexpectedly taken place in the kingdom of Poland constitute a serious threat to public and private *property* and may also

affect the interests of public order, commerce and industry in the neighbouring Prussian provinces, have agreed:

That on the demand of the Commander in Chief of the Russian army in the kingdom of Poland or of the General of Infantry Werder, commanding the first, second, fifth and sixth Prussian army corps, or of the neighbouring authorities of the two countries, the commanders of Russian and Prussian detachments shall be authorised to hold themselves ready for mutual cooperation, and in case of need to cross the border in order to pursue the rebels who pass from one country to another. Special officers shall be sent by both sides, for service in the headquarters of the two armies and with the commanding officers of the detachments, with a view to the practical execution of this agreement. These officers will be kept informed of any military redeployment so as to be able to communicate them to their respective commanding officers.

Secret article:

It has been agreed with Prince Gorchakov that any signs of political intrigues relating to the Grand Duchy of Posen shall be transmitted by him directly to Berlin and communicated by the head of the diplomatic chancellery at Warsaw to the Prussian officer destined to reside in that town, who will pass them on to General Werder.

APP, iii, 231-2

(ii) *Bismarck to Alvensleben, telegram, 7 February 1863*

The King authorizes you to sign the two articles in your telegram of 6th. His Majesty agrees to the second article remaining secret but wishes it to be re-worded so as to constitute a reciprocal obligation on the part of the two governments in regard to the communications that they mutually undertake to make to each other.

APP, iii, 232-3

5   Russell Remonstrates over the Alvensleben Convention

Earl Russell to Sir A. Buchanan, despatch, 2 March 1863

SIR,
The Convention which has been concluded between Russia and

Prussia, relation to the affairs of Poland, has caused considerable uneasiness in this country.

The Powers of Europe were disposed to be neutral in the contest between the Russian Government and the Polish insurgents.

Prussia has departed from this course.

My inquiries, as well as a despatch from Lord Napier, have led me to believe that the Convention contains:

1. An agreement that Russian troops, upon crossing the frontier of Prussia, shall not be disarmed, as would be required according to international usage, but shall be allowed to retain their arms, and to remain, and to act as an armed body in Prussian territory.

2. A permission for Russian troops to pursue and capture Polish insurgents on Prussian territory.

Count Bernstorff defended this Convention, and declared that it was not an engagement invoking intervention in the contest between Russia and the Poles.

But it is clear that if Russian troops are to be at liberty to follow and attack the Polish insurgents in Prussian territory, the Prussian Government makes itself a party to the war now raging in Poland.

If Great Britain were to allow a Federal ship-of-war to attack a Confederate ship in British waters, Great Britain would become a party to the war between the Federal Government of the The United States and the Confederate.

It is obvious that by this Convention Prussia engages to become a party in the war against the Poles without any apparent necessity for so doing. For Her Majesty's Government have not heard that any disaffection prevails in the Polish provinces of Prussia.

It is but too probable that this Convention will irritate the Polish subjects of Prussia, tend to excite disaffection where it has not hitherto existed, and thus extend the insurrection.

Upon viewing this Convention in all its aspects, therefore, Her Majesty's Government are forced to arrive at the conclusion that it is an act of intervention which is not justified by necessity; which will tend to alienate the affections of the Polish subjects of the King of Prussia; and which, indirectly, gives support and countenance to the arbitrary conscription of Warsaw.

You will read this despatch to M. Bismarck, and you will ask for a copy of the Convention between Prussia and Russia.

It is possible that the Governments of Prussia and Russia, aware of the objections to which this Convention is liable, and seeing the ill consequences it may produce, may be disposed to cancel it, or to put an end to its operation.

In that case you will inform me what steps have been taken with that view.

I am, etc. RUSSELL

BFSP, 1862-3, pp. 807-8

6   Bismarck seeks closer Russo-Prussian relations, September 1863

Oubril (Berlin) to Gorchakov, despatch no. 297, 3/15 September 1863

[Bismarck spoke at length on German affairs, and was indignant at Austria's conduct.] 'What moreover has been Austria's attitude towards us? We have been trying since last winter to draw near to her and it was only when we offered her our hand that she took advantage of it to deliver the most palpable blow that she has ever dared to aim at us. Even before Olmütz she never dreamed of so bold a stroke. . . .

So we have made our decisions and we shall act accordingly. Warn Prince Gorchakov of this and draw his attention to the gravity of the situation. You are accustomed to a Prussia leading a tranquil existence between Berlin and Sans-Souci and going when necessary to Olmütz. These times are definitely passed; I advise you of this in all seriousness.'

. . . I replied to the President of the Council that I recognized that Prussia could not accept the Austrian proposals; that she could declare this in her replies; but that between there and the beginning of a campaign there was some distance to go; that in my view the right course would be merely to state the position and allow the fantastic scaffolding of Frankfort to collapse; that without alliances war was a sorry undertaking, as we had ourselves experienced only too often; that finally the king would probably not wish to push matters so far.

'The king' replied M. de Bismarck, 'is a soldier'—which, in his mind, probably meant that His Majesty recognized or would recognize the necessity for prompt and vigorous action. 'As to alliances, he added, we shall find them. We had always counted on you. The Emperor Alexander once said: The policy of Russia and Prussia must be one and the same. We have drawn inspiration from this idea.—I myself am the representative of the Russian alliance—it is my banner; it is my *raison d'être*; I should be the first to give way to a Liberal minister, even a Progressive, if we were to have the sad experience of finding ourselves mistaken—about you. Look at it from your own standpoint if it suits you, but in my opinion there ought to be parity of policy, and I doubt whether regard for, or an abstention on your part in favour of Austria can profit you much. Why have you 300,000 men on your frontiers? Is it on account of a few Polish bands? Or have you only called them up just to send them back to their homes? Think of this seriously, but above all tell the Prince that a little forceful language in Vienna will doubtless have a salutary effect and prevent many calamities. . . .'

I told Bismarck that our 300,000 men were intended to safeguard the empire from foreign threats, but that we had declared that we had no aggressive hostilities against anyone in view. I then reassured him as to our goodwill towards Prussia, which we would like to see strong and powerful and which we recognize will play a large part in the destiny of Germany. . . . I added that our observations only rested on an apprehension, nevertheless very real, that there might be active interference by the Emperor Napoleon in the affairs of Germany, if hostilities should break out between Prussia and Austria. In our opinion that was a consideration which must not be lost sight of.

'Very well', replied M. de Bismarck, 'let him interfere, it will not frighten us. It is a risk we must run. In any case there is no way of securing the disinterest of France. One thing must be taken into account; that is, that the line of the Weser is more important to us than that of the Rhine. That, in short, is the question.'

APP. iii, no. 693

7 Von der Goltz reprimanded

Bismarck to Graf Robert von der Goltz, 24 December 1863

. . . As regards the Danish affair, it is not possible for the King to have two foreign ministers, i.e. that in the most decisive question of the day the most important diplomatic post should advocate directly to the King a policy at variance with the ministerial one. The friction in our state machine, already excessive, cannot be intensified. I will tolerate opposition, if it emanates from a competent source such as yourself; but the advising of the King in this matter I will share officially with no one, and if H.M. were to demand that of me, I should resign from my post. I told H.M. that when reading him your latest reports. H.M. found my point of view a natural one, and I can only adhere to it. No one expects reports which reflect only ministerial views; but yours are not reports in the usual sense, but assume the nature of ministerial

pronouncements, which recommend to the King a completely contradictory policy to the one which he himself decided on in council
with the whole ministry, and which he has in fact carried out for the
last month. Criticism of this resolution, which I would call sharp if not
downright hostile, does not constitute an ambassadorial report, but a
quite different ministerial programme. Such cross points of view can
only do *harm* and no good; for it can arouse hesitation and indecision,
and in my opinion any policy is better than a vacillating one.

I utterly repudiate your remark that an 'in itself very simple question
of Prussian policy' is obscured by the dust that the Danish affair is
raising and the phantasmagoria associated with it. The question is
whether we are a great power or a German federal state, and whether
we, in accordance with the first conception are to be ruled monarchi-
cally or, as is possible in the second case, by professors, district judges
and provincial gossips. The chase after the phantom of popularity
'in Germany', which we have been pursuing since the forties, has cost
us our position in Germany and in Europe, and we shall not regain it
by drifting with the current with the idea of guiding it, but only by
standing firmly on our own feet and being *firstly* a great power, and
only secondly a federal state. Austria, to our detriment, has always
recognised that with reference to herself, and she will not allow herself
to be wrested from her European alliances, if she has any, by the farce
which she is playing out with German sympathies. . . .

GW, xiv(ii), p. 658

8   A Hint to France about the Rhine Frontiers, December 1863

General Count Fleury (Berlin), to Napoleon III, telegram, 24 December 1863

Very lengthy first interview with M. de Bismarck. He is satisfied with
the assurances I gave him regarding the Danish attitude, but it is important that the French Cabinet considers this in the light of my
despatch from Copenhagen, i.e. withdrawal of the Constitution before
1st January. On this condition alone will Prussia be in a position to
impose moderation on the Confederation [and] prevent a compromising conflict, in other words war, that must be avoided now at
all costs. It might well be the subject of negotiations if one wants a
congress.

And now an important aspect of the question. M. de Bismarck says that the Congress ought to be restricted to the matter of the Duchies. To expect a restricted congress to deal with general affairs is impossible. Prussia and Russia would no longer attend it, nor England and Austria. Better to die, said M. de Bismarck, than to let others discuss our possessions in Posen. I would sooner cede our Rhenish provinces! But the Minister is confident of being able to bring to the special Congress all the powers who are interested signatories: England, Russia, Austria, etc. The reunion would take place in Paris, to satisfy the Emperor.

This would be the first stage, the point past which we have to get the King [of Prussia], who is very timorous confronted by his family of Princes and Princesses, very sentimental towards Austria on the German question, but again very scared by the Polish question and French opinion on this subject. M. de Bismarck himself would lose all his power *vis-à-vis* Germany if he did not side with Austria in the German question.

Nothing ultimately possible then if one does not start with the Danish affair. Everything will follow from that, and situations will emerge.

As to plans for aggrandizement, of preponderance at the expense of Austria, that is understood. As to the frontiers of the Rhine, the word has been spoken. Is it necessary to emphasize it further?

But to come to terms with the King, in a word, to form an alliance, the only chance is to have the Danish Congress. . . .

As to Russia, nothing can be achieved by making a great fuss, as the Emperor thought. Reconciliation will come about solely by sending another ambassador in place of Montebello, who no longer has any authority.

OD, i, 2-4

9   Bismarck asserts Prussia's Disinterest in the Danish Question

Baron Talleyrand (Berlin), to Drouyn de Lhuys (French foreign minister), 9 February 1864

Despatch no. 25
[Questions Bismarck concerning reports that Prince of Augustenburg has been proclaimed Duke of Schleswig throughout areas occupied by Austro-Prussian

troops. Bismarck ascribes this to partisans, and has asked Marshal Wrangel for explanations.]

'In reality, Baron Bismarck told me, I do not know what the Marshal writes to the King. This correspondence is withheld from me, and I have had to consult my colleagues in the Council as to the attitude we should take *vis-à-vis* the Prince of Augustenburg. He possesses the secret sympathy of the King, and has openly acquired that of the Crown Prince. The presence of the heir to the throne in Schleswig, his speeches and his behaviour, impair more and more the unity of government action.

'As to myself, my ideas on the Danish question have not changed. Of all the policies which can be followed, the most inept for Prussia would be to concur in the setting up of a German Grand Duchy, and to create a prince who, in time of peace, would vote against us at Frankfurt, and in time of war would compromise us, if not betray us. Believe me, it is not for a *contemptible fellow* like the Prince of Augustenburg that Prussia expends the blood of its soldiers and the money of its coffers. The incorporation in Prussia of two such fine provinces is ready made to tempt our ambition; but, of all sovereigns, the King is perhaps the most disinterested, and besides, he knows that the other powers would not consent to an aggrandizement of territory for him without some compensation. There remains therefore the agreement with Denmark: that is what I desire and in view of that I adhere to the principle of the integrity of that monarchy. Nevertheless the task is arduous, and it will be more difficult to satisfy Germany than to lead King Christian IX to a settlement. I have no illusions as to the result at which I shall arrive. If I fail in my policy, I shall be accused of folly; if I succeed, I shall be accused of treason.'

I could reassure the Minister only against the first of these alternatives. . . .

OD, i, 280-2

10   Augustenburg refuses Prussia's Terms

Bismarck's record of conversation with Augustenburg, 3 June 1864

I had hoped to find the Prince of Augustenburg in a frame of mind to accept gratefully our very moderate demands, and met him with this in mind, when he visited me at about 9 o'clock on the evening of 1st inst.

I said that he was our candidate; we would like an understanding with him in case we could get his succession universally recognized. Our main interest was the German one, not the dynastic; the greatest possible severing of links with Denmark; that we would be ready to devote our efforts on his behalf on certain conditions which would be commensurate with consideration of our own nation, whom we could not confront with empty hands after a bloody campaign.

He asked what our demands were.

I referred to the six points in the letter to H.M. the King [Prince Friedrich's letter to King William of 29 April] adding that they could perhaps be simplified by combining marine establishments and fortifications in the shape of a ship canal from Echernförde to Brunsbüttel with two fortified terminals on the two seas; it was a military question whether the Eckenförde fortification could take the place of the costly building of still another Bund fortification at Rendsburg.

I would only need to add:

1. that if the planned establishments could not be installed in good time as Bund institutions, the Duke would declare himself ready to relinquish the two terminals to Prussia after the analogy of Jahde Bay, in which case we should come to an understanding with the Bund over the whole system of coastal protection; likewise the right to inspect the canal in the same way as a State railway.

2. a military convention, containing a naval convention, to the effect that the number of troops to be in the service of the Prussian fleet should be deducted from the land contingent.

On all these points the Prince made difficulties.

... He could only go before the Landtag with such conditions if he could keep all the duchies or at least the boundary from Gjenner Bay north of Apenrade, otherwise not. He could not accept insulting conditions. By these he meant: a more southerly boundary than that specified; taking over debts for war costs and in addition cessions of territory;—he could not face the Landtag and the people with that kind of plan.

In the discussion he emphasized that we would do better to win his heart than bind him to firm commitments; then he could carry out Prussian policy.

I answered that we had hoped to have won his heart already.

Finally he explained that he wanted to think over the matter in Dolzig, and that he looked on this, only as a discussion for mutual clarification of the situation. . . .

11   France Renounces Intervention in Denmark, June 1864

Drouyn de Lhuys to Prince de la Tour d'Auvergne (London), 27 June 1864

... We accordingly felt that our position as a neighbour state of Germany, as well as the principles of our public policy, called for extreme reserve on our part. Nothing in the events which have taken place hitherto have shown that this course was not at the same time both the most equitable and the most wise.

We recognize, however, that the resumption of hostilities profoundly changes the respective positions of the belligerents. In continuing the war, the German powers are no longer defending the rights of the Germanic populations of the Duchies; they threaten the independence of the Danish populations, and may be led to do serious harm to the equilibrium of the north. We could certainly not view such eventualities with indifference. They do not however affect us directly enough to warrant our intervention in a struggle which would exact from us efforts of which it would be impossible to predict the extent. We should be constrained to devote all means of action to it, and it would be the duty of the government of the Emperor to the people of France not to lay down arms without claiming, as a reward for its sacrifices, compensations which could lead to important changes in the territorial boundaries, and consequently also modifications in the present state of the general balance of power. We would like to reject all thought of enterprises of this nature as long as we are not constrained by the most obvious necessity of following a different policy, and we do not believe that circumstances, although already very serious, oblige us at present to depart from the neutrality that we wish to preserve.

We understand, however, that the English government, whose situation is very different from ours, and who has, from the very first, lent in consequence a more forceful character to its language and its actions, should now take too a more active attitude. And it can, if it judges it opportune, take part in the hostilities without involving the whole continent in war. Powerful considerations may make it decide to adopt this expedient. The Danish cause, in this new phase caused by the breaking-off of negotiations, has a right to the sympathy which we have never refused to an ancient ally, and in lending it her support, the British government will not only not have to fear any opposition or any difficulty on the part of France, but will be able to count on the benevolent character of the neutrality which will be observed by the Emperor's government. I have had numerous opportunities recently of making known my feelings on this subject to Lord Cowley. . . .

OD, iii, 284-5

C

SETTLING ACCOUNTS WITH AUSTRIA, 1864-1866

The treaty of Vienna was for Bismarck the successful completion of a stage in his campaign for Prussian supremacy in Germany; the final settlement with Austria had still to come. Irritated and somewhat abashed by her complete failure to influence the outcome, Britain was not disposed to interfere if the two conquerors of Denmark quarrelled over the spoils, although she, like Russia, was uneasy at the prospect of increased French interference in Germany. Yet British inaction left Napoleon correspondingly freer to seek the successes and the consequent prestige for which he hankered, and Bismarck was sufficiently forthcoming to keep alive French hopes for gains towards Belgium, Luxemburg, and even the Rhineland. No one had any inclination to harass Prussia. Austria on the other hand had challenges elsewhere. Magyar home rule, Serbian and Italian irredentism, the embarrassing possibilities of a Franco-Russian clash over Rumania, the unfinished Polish crisis and chronic financial stringency made a single-minded concentration on the struggle for supremacy in Germany impossible for her.

There was much to be said therefore from Austria's point of view for continuing the experiment of Austro-Prussian collaboration in German affairs, and Bismarck in his arrogant but circumspect style was prepared to exploit the collaboration to the limit of Austria's capacity for concession (1). War as an alternative was being prepared but was not accepted as inevitable for the time being. If it did become necessary in Bismarck's view the final decision would depend on the readiness of the General Staff for action, and on Bismarck's ability to persuade King William to overcome his reluctance to fight, or to make up his mind.

At the Schönbrunn meeting late in August 1864 King William, questioned by the Emperor Franz Joseph, disclaimed any right to the duchies, and this enabled Bismarck to evade Rechberg's proposal that Prussia should support Austria in recovering Lombardy in return for an outright Prussian annexation of Schleswig-Holstein. The Prussian government would not even hold out any hope of future consideration for Austria's case over the Zollverein, although it seems that Bismarck himself was not opposed to some innocuous concession. Rechberg resigned on 27 October 1864, and was succeeded by the inexperienced Count Mensdorff, who relied greatly on an influential foreign office official, Baron von Biegeleben. Biegeleben favoured a tougher line with Prussia, but Mensdorff got little change out of Bismarck when he proposed in November either a new state under Augustenburg or Prussian annexation of the duchies with compensation for Austria in Silesia and elsewhere. Bismarck talked a good deal, but his definite answer was delayed until February 1865, when he accepted the Augustenburg plan only on terms which would have meant the virtual annexation of the new state by Prussia. After Austria early in April had appealed defiantly to the diet in favour of Augustenburg, Prussia announced on 5 April the transfer of the chief Prussian naval station from Danzig to Kiel.

War seemed probable. King William now appeared agreeable to annexation and the army was ready to fight. It was undoubtedly Bismarck's influence which at this point postponed the breach with Austria, partly it would seem because he was still hoping to get all he wanted from her without war, partly because his plans for taking over the *Bund* were not complete. After prolonged tension a compromise was patched up in the Convention of Gastein of 14 August 1865 (2). Given the determination of Prussia to secure complete control of the duchies the provision for shared administration, Prussia in Schleswig and Austria in Holstein, was disastrous for Austria; she had abandoned Augustenburg while Prussia retained joint sovereignty, with lines of communication and military establishments in Holstein which gave her ample powers of annoyance. A circular from the French foreign minister, Drouyn de Lhuys, to the French diplomatic agents abroad denounced the Gastein Convention as having no foundation other than force, and no justification other than the reciprocal convenience of the two co-partners. The real cause of this sharp French reaction was that the terms seemed so favourable to Prussia as to suggest some secret Prussian compensatory concession to Austria, probably in Italy. Napoleon also undoubtedly felt alarm at the prospect of an Austro-Prussian agreement which would increase his own isolation and diminish his chance of future profit from the German situation. Bismarck felt it expedient to keep alive the French hopes of compensation; he had talks with the Emperor at Biarritz in October 1865, and it seems likely that he reassured Napoleon on this point, without making any definite commitment (3).

The Austrian government seemed for the moment to be more hopeful than its neutral critics, and it was Bismarck who, after the end of 1865, took the lead in preparing a showdown which faced Austria with the final choice of surrender or war. Apart from the intractable nature of Austro-Prussian tension in the duchies, Austria had to take into account the ambitions of France and Italy. Assured by the Prussian chief of staff, von Moltke, that an Italian military diversion was essential when Austria and Prussia fought, Bismarck on 8 April concluded the Italian-Prussian treaty whereby Italy undertook to join the war against Austria if it broke out within three months. This in the event of a Prussian victory would mean Italy's acquisition of Venetia, and would presumably please Napoleon, pledged to Italian independence. But would he also find it expedient to interfere directly in the war? It was a reasonable guess that he would be content to stand aside and seek advantages from the situation after the two had exhausted themselves in battle.

Bismarck's moves up to this point are well documented as far as his exchanges with Austria go; he continually harped on his loyalty to the Russian cause and the conservative principle, and had no difficulty in keeping the slightly patronizing goodwill of the tsar and Gorchakov; his bargaining with the Italians was mercenary and frank. Only in his delicate cultivation of Napoleon's temporizing goodwill is there some ambiguity, for while Napoleon could never commit himself finally to demands in the Rhineland, Bismarck did not intend to exclude the possibility so harshly as to produce an open breach. Early in March 1866 King William sounded Napoleon as to a closer entente (4); the emperor at first declared his neutrality, then appeared during April and May to be angling for concessions in the Rhineland, and finally resumed his non-committal stance. He sought instead to satisfy French interests by reviving the plan for a congress to settle outstanding European issues peacefully; the other four powers as usual looked on it with distrust, but Mensdorff was responsible for its rejection at the end of May. But he had to make the best terms with Napoleon he could by the Franco-Austrian agreement of 12 June whereby in the event of war Austria would cede Venetia to France and France promised not to oppose Austrian acquisitions in Germany only if these 'did not disturb the European equilibrium'.

Sir Robert Morier's diatribe on the eve of war (5) is a reminder that in the liberal or constitutional sphere Bismarck was now widely detested, both in Germany and elsewhere. As a diplomatist he was as yet less appreciated and less feared. To many in Paris and elsewhere who believed that Austria would probably triumph in a war his conduct appeared to lack finesse and even sense. Although he had been trying to goad Austria into war since the beginning of the year he wished her to appear the aggressor in order (among other things) to satisfy King William's conscience, and some Austrian gestures (such as her mobilization in March) put her in the wrong in other eyes than the king's. But, being cautious as well as bold, Bismarck kept open almost to the last the possibility of a peaceful settlement on a *kleindeutsch* basis (with Prussian predominance north of the Main), proposed by Anton von Gablenz.[1] Rapid military victory in the 'three weeks war', with the decisive battle fought at Sadowa (or Königgrätz) on 3 July, now, however, put his judgment in a more favourable light.

After Sadowa the problem was again to reassure his two powerful neighbours, France and Russia, without abandoning his essential aims in the peace settlement. Napoleon's immediate intervention, proposing in effect an armistice on 4 July (6) was an attempt to dominate the situation which Bismarck took in his stride, although he later professed his annoyance. He was quite willing to bring the war to a speedy end on his own terms; the Prussian army continued to advance for some days, but the Austrians agreed to the preliminary peace treaty of Nikolsburg on 26 July, following an armistice of five days concluded

[1] Otto Becker, *Bismarcks Ringen um Deutschlands Gestaltung*, pp. 121-59.

at noon on 22 July. The decisive moment had come on 9 July, when Bismarck instructed Goltz to sound Napoleon as to the annexation by Prussia of most of the German states north of the Main. There is evidence that he was preparing to accept a much less ambitious programme: on 8 July he had told Schweinitz to assure the tsar that the reform of the *Bund* and the expulsion of Austria without extensive Prussian annexations were the crux of the matter for him. Napoleon demanded the cession of Venetia by Austria and objected to any annexation of Austrian or Saxon territory by Prussia; but otherwise he made no objection to Bismarck's north German programme, which Bismarck promptly interpreted in terms of the complete incorporation of certain north German states. He acquiesced in the French desire to exclude the German states south of the river Main, which were to join together if they wished to form an independent union of south Germany: he did not feel strong enough to force these states into his north German confederation at this time. The detailed French terms were put forward by Drouyn de Lhuys on 14 July (**7**), and Bismarck's more ambitious plans for north Germany were telegraphed to St. Petersburg on the 17th. The drastic change in his attitude embarrassed Schweinitz, although he found the tsar less upset by it than he had feared.

Nevertheless it seemed abundantly clear to Bismarck that the sensible thing was to clinch matters with Austria on the basis of the French terms as swiftly as possible, in spite of the hostility of the Prussian generals, which King William shared, to this relatively lenient course. Bismarck marshalled the arguments in the masterly 'Nikolsburg' memorandum of 24 July (**8**), but secured the king's agreement only after tears, recriminations, and thoughts of suicide on his part. He was, however, helped by the intervention of the Crown Prince. The armistice was signed with Austria at Nikolsburg on 26 July.

Would the other powers agree? Neither France nor Russia was happy about the new arrangements, but their reasons differed and did not provide a basis for joint action. France accepted Bismarck's plans, but wanted territorial compensation, something for herself; Russia did not seek compensation in that sense, and the rather cloudy objections of Gorchakov and the tsar were due to desire to be consulted and to uneasiness about the consequences of the new arrangements rather than a desire to alter them. Gorchakov proposed a congress and this unwelcome suggestion was put to Prussia on 27 July; it was subsequently accepted by the French government and rejected by the British. The tsar, however, was pleased when King William sent his eminent general, Edwin von Manteuffel, to explain things. Manteuffel reached St. Petersburg on 9 August. Bismarck's sense of timing told him that further temporization was inadvisable; after receiving Manteuffel's first report he threatened to meet foreign interference with a desperate revolutionary policy, and to appeal to Germany by proclaiming the constitution of 1849. A day or two later Gorchakov told the French ambassador that Russia had abandoned serious thoughts of a congress or of protest against Bismarck's arrangements.

Before this, on 5 August, Drouyn had at last presented definite demands. France wanted the 1814 frontier, the Bavarian left bank of the Rhine as far as

Mainz, and the abandonment of all Prussian links with Limburg and Luxembourg (9). Bismarck professed to be shocked by the extent of these demands (10). As France was not prepared to enforce them by war she could do no more than advance diminished proposals in subsequent months which Bismarck was in no hurry to discuss. The definitive Austro-Prussian peace treaty was signed at Prague on 23 August 1866 (11).

1   Prospects of Austro-Prussian Alliance, 1864

Le Comte de Salignac-Fénelon (Frankfurt) to Drouyn de Lhuys, 9 September 1864

[He reports some comments by Bismarck in a conversation with an acquaintance at Baden on 3 September.] Our cabinet is on the first step of a growing alliance with Austria. The commercial dispute is only a secondary detail. You know that Austria has renounced her original demands, and that we are hastening to make an arrangement that will give her some semblance of satisfaction and facilitate an honourable retreat. I humour her a bit on this point, so that she may leave me a freer hand in the Duchies. For the rest, we are agreed on the main principles, and if some new incident should momentarily raise some discussion between us, it will only be a passing difference of opinion, and of short duration. In all important matters, we march and shall march in step. It is not, as someone has suggested, that we have already signed a treaty [of alliance]. We have no obligations, for example, towards Italy. What is being said about the Mincio line and the Treaty of Zürich is pure invention. But a firm rapprochement has been brought about. We do not want to receive any more peremptory pronouncements from the Court of the Tuileries.

At the moment our chief desire is to get the most we can out of the war with Denmark. We shall accept a Schleswig port, the Duchy of Lauenburg, or anything they let us take. This will be a starting-point, and *the rest will follow in due course*. The mission of Prussia is to expand. We must always keep that in mind. Our aims must be vast, and have a wide horizon. . . .

OD, iv, no. 837

2   Gastein Convention between Austria and Prussia, 14 August 1865

Article I. The exercise of the Rights acquired in common by the High Contracting Parties, in virtue of Article III of the Vienna Treaty of

Peace of 30th October, 1864, shall, without prejudice to the continuance of those rights of both Powers to the whole of both Duchies, pass to His Majesty the Emperor of Austria as regards the Duchy of Holstein, and to His Majesty the King of Prussia as regards the Duchy of Schleswig.

Article II. The High Contracting Parties will propose to the Diet the establishment of a German Fleet, and will fix upon the Harbour of Kiel as a Federal Harbour for the said Fleet.

Until the resolutions of the Diet with respect to this proposal have been carried into effect, the Ships of War of both Powers shall use this Harbour, and the Command and the Police Duties within it shall be exercised by Prussia. Prussia is entitled both to establish the necessary Fortifications opposite Friedrichsort for the protection of the entrance, and also to fit up along the Holstein bank of the inlet the Naval Establishments that are requisite in a Military Port. These Fortifications and Establishments remain likewise under Prussian command, and the Prussian marines and troops required for their Garrison and Protection may be quartered in Kiel and the neighbourhood.

Article III. The High Contracting Parties will propose in Frankfort the elevation of Rendsburg into a German Federal Fortress.

Until the Diet shall have issued the regulations respecting Garrisoning the said Fortress, the Garrison shall consist of Imperial Austrian and Royal Prussian troops under a command annually alternating on the 1st July.

Article IV. While the division agreed upon in Article I of the present Convention continues, the Royal Prussian Government shall retain two Military Roads through Holstein; the one from Lubeck to Kiel, the other from Hamburg to Rendsburg.

All details as to the Military Stations, and as to the transport and subsistence of the Troops, shall be regulated as soon as possible in a Special Convention. Until this has been done, the Regulations in force as to the Prussian Military Roads through Hanover shall be observed.

Article V. [Prussia retains the disposal of one telegraphic wire for communication with Kiel and Rendsburg. She will in due course request the granting of the concession for a railway from Lubeck through Kiel to Schleswig.]

Article VI. [The duchies shall in due course enter the Zollverein.]

Article VII. Prussia is entitled to make the Canal that is to be cut between the North Sea and the Baltic, through the Territory of Holstein, according to the result of the professional investigations undertaken by the Prussian Government. . . .

Article VIII. [Stipulations of the Treaty of Vienna relative to the financial obligations of the duchies will remain unaltered.]

Article IX. His Majesty the Emperor of Austria cedes to His Majesty the King of Prussia the Rights acquired in the aforementioned Vienna Treaty of Peace with respect to the Duchy of Lauenburg; and in return the Royal Prussian Government binds itself to pay to the Austrian Government the sum of 2,500,000 Danish rix-dollars, payable at Berlin in Prussian silver, 4 weeks after confirmation of the present Convention by their Majesties the Emperor of Austria and the King of Prussia.

Article X. The carrying into effect of the foregoing division of the Co-Sovereignty, which has been agreed upon, shall begin as soon as possible after the approval of this Convention by their Majesties the Emperor of Austria and the King of Prussia, and shall be accomplished at the latest by the 15th September.

The joint Command-in-Chief, hitherto existing, shall be dissolved on the complete Evacuation of Holstein by the Prussian troops and of Schleswig by the Austrian troops, by the 15th September, at the latest. . . .

> (L.S.) G. BLOME
> (L.S.) VON BISMARCK
> Hertslet, iii, no. 370

3   The Biarritz Meeting, 1865

Bismarck to King William I, 11 October 1865

. . . The day after my arrival in Biarritz I was received by the Emperor in special audience. . . . It was evident that the Emperor himself fervently wished that the Circular of 29 August could be undone. He did not seem to know that I was aware of his previous approval of it, for he emphasized that while he took personal charge of foreign matters in important situations, he did not concern himself much about details of ordinary business, unless he was made aware of their significance. . . . In this way they had exaggerated in Paris the importance of the Gastein agreement for the general policy of Prussia, especially as they could not believe that a result which was so advantageous to Prussia had not been purchased by some secret concessions to Austria. The

Emperor let it be seen (as Drouyn de Lhuys had already pointed out to me in no uncertain terms) that the Austrian communication, which had reached him by very confidential channels (apparently through Her Majesty the Empress) had supported the hypothesis of a secret understanding of the German powers, directed as a sort of coalition against France. Again His Majesty solemnly put the question to me, whether we had not given Austria some guarantee about Venetia. I denied it . . .; moreover, I thought it impossible that we would conclude an agreement in the future whereby Austria could make a war in which Prussia would have to join without advantage to herself. The Emperor thereupon assured me that he did not intend to initiate any plans which might disturb the peace of Europe. . . . Using almost the very words in which I had voiced the [same] sentiment to Minister Drouyn de Lhuys, and which the latter had doubtless passed on meanwhile, he said: one must not seek to fashion events, but let them mature of themselves; they would not fail to happen, and would then prove that Prussia and France were the two states in Europe whose interests were bound up with one another to the greatest degree, and that he would always be ready to give practical proof of the sympathy and friendship he felt for Prussia.—The Emperor then asked what arrangement we proposed to come to with Austria over Holstein. I answered frankly that we hoped to secure and keep Holstein by paying an indemnity. His Majesty made no objection to this, and expressly declared his agreement with the reasons I gave for refuting the anxiety of Minister Drouyn de Lhuys concerning the growth of Prussian power without any equivalent for France. I emphasized the point that the acquisition of the Elbe Duchies was not in itself a strengthening of Prussian power; on the contrary, by deploying our navy and developing our defensive position northwards it would tie up the forces of our Fatherland in more than one direction to an extent which would not be compensated by the addition of a million inhabitants.

H. v. Sybel, *Die Begründung des Deutschen Reiches durch Wilhelm I* (Munich, 1890), iv, 215-18

4 King William offers Napoleon a closer Entente

William I to Napoleon III, 3 March 1866 [draft in Bismarck's hand]

When last year my Minister for Foreign Affairs had the honour of being received by Your Majesty at Biarritz and St. Cloud, you were good enough to charge him to inform me that You, like myself, were of the opinion that, in order to agree on the future of our political relations, it was important not to precipitate the development of the situation, but to await its progress and adapt our resolutions to it. And to the statement of Your opinion Your Majesty added an invitation to write to You confidentially, as soon as circumstances seemed to me to indicate the need for a closer and more special entente between our two governments. I feel the moment has come, and guided by the recollection of the assurances of political sympathy and personal friendship which Your Majesty gave me on that occasion, I have instructed Count von der Goltz to lay before You, with all the frankness and loyalty which have always governed our mutual relations, my own views on the present situation in Europe, and the attitude which in my opinion must consequently be taken by Prussia. If Your Majesty would be good enough to let me know Your reaction to the proposals which my ambassador will submit to you, I beg you to believe that I shall receive the communications You send with all the discretion consistent with the personal character which Your Majesty is good enough to bestow on this exchange of ideas.

> H. Oncken, *Die Rheinpolitik*
> *Kaiser Napoleons III 1863 bis*
> *1870* (Berlin, 1926), i, 92-3

5 An English Liberal judges Bismarck, 1866

Sir Robert Morier, Vienna, to Lady Salisbury, 24 June 1866

... The one thing for which, ... above all other things, I conceive Bismarck ought to be execrated, is his having by the impress of his own detestable individuality on the political canvas now unrolling before Europe so utterly disfigured the true outlines of the picture, that not only public opinion, but the judgment of wise and thoughtful men is almost sure to go wrong. I say this quite deliberately, knowing that if Bismarck succeeds the world will clap its hands and say he was the only man who knew how to bring about what the world, which always worships success, will say was a consummation it always desired. Whereas that which will be really proved is that Prussia was so strong and so really the heart and head and lungs of Germany, that she could, by her mere natural development *with*, instead of *against*, the liberal and national forces of Germany, have effected what required to be done by peaceful means and without bloodshed. If, on the other hand, Austria succeeds and Prussia is crushed, the world will clap its hands and say Prussia was a parvenu snob that required putting down, and German unity an absurd Utopia. . .

Memoirs and Letters of Sir Robert
Morier (London, 1911), ii, 71-2

6 Napoleon demands an Armistice after Königgrätz

Napoleon III to William I, 4 July 1866

Your Majesty's swift and brilliant victories have led to results which force me to depart from my role of complete abstention. The Emperor of Austria has informed me that he will cede me Venetia and that he is ready to accept my mediation to end the conflict which has arisen between Austria, Prussia and Italy. I know too well Your Majesty's feelings of magnanimity and affectionate trust in me not to believe that, after having raised so high the honour of your arms, Your Majesty will accept with satisfaction the efforts which I am disposed to make to aid you to restore to your lands and to Europe the precious benefits of peace.

If Your Majesty agrees to my proposition, you will no doubt deem it proper that an armistice between Germany and Italy will immediately pave the way for these negotiations.

OD, x, 4

7 French Terms for a Settlement

Drouyn de Lhuys to Benedetti, 14 July 1866

I am taking advantage of the hurried departure of the Marquis de la Coste to acquaint you with the preliminaries of peace which His Majesty is recommending Prussia and Austria to accept.

The integrity of the Austrian Empire, apart from Venetia, shall be maintained.

Austria will recognize the dissolution of the old Germanic Confederation, and will not oppose a new organisation of Germany, of which she will not be a member.

Prussia will establish a union of northern Germany, comprising all the states situated north of the Main. She will be invested with the command of the military forces of these states.

The German states situated south of the Main will be free to form amongst themselves a union of South Germany, which will enjoy an independent international existence.

The national links to be maintained between the northern union and that of the south will be freely regulated by a common entente.

The Elbe Duchies shall be reunited with Prussia, except those districts of northern Schleswig whose populations, freely consulted, desire to be retroceded to Denmark.

Austria and her allies will repay Prussia a part of the costs of the war.

If these fundamental principles were adopted by the belligerent parties, an armistice could be concluded immediately, and the way would be open to the reestablishment of an equitable and lasting peace.

Use every effort to persuade Prussia to accept these proposals.

OD, ii, 30-2

8   The Nikolsburg Memorandum, 24 July 1866

Regarding the negotiations with Austria to find a basis for peace, I respectfully beg Your Majesty to allow me to lay before you the following considerations:

It seems to me of the greatest importance that the present favourable moment should not be missed. [*William I*: Agreed.] By Your Majesty's declared acceptance *en bloc* of the proposals of His Majesty the Emperor of the French, the danger of France's taking sides against Prussia, which by diplomatic pressure could easily turn into active participation, has been eliminated. [*William I*: Correct.] As a result of the instructions given to Count Goltz on Your Majesty's orders, it has been possible to secure in addition from the Emperor Napoleon the definite assurance, as Count Goltz reported telegraphically on 22 inst., that he will not only allow the direct annexation of 4 million in N. Germany, but will himself recommend it, without any mention being made of compensation for France. [*William I*: Correct.] But the wavering of the Emperor in the last few weeks, and the pressure of public opinion in France, raise definite fears that, if the present concessions are not quickly converted into fact, then there could be a new *volte-face*. We cannot count on support from the other great powers for further, or even these, Prussian demands. Your Majesty has observed in the letters of H.M. the Emperor of Russia with what alarm he views the Prussian conditions. His Minister, Prince Gortschakow, has also expressed the wish to know these conditions, both through Your Majesty's ambassador in St Petersburg and Baron Oubril in Berlin. [*William I*: Russia's proposal for a congress is already evidence of this, for Russia will use this to oppose the peace preliminaries.] The family connexions of the Russian Imperial house with German dynasties give rise to the fear that in further negotiations sympathy with them will carry great weight. In England, public opinion begins to veer towards Your Majesty's military victories: but the same cannot be said of the government, and it can only be assumed that it will recognize the *faits accomplis*.

The double declaration of Austria that it will withdraw from the German Bund and agree to a reconstruction of it under Prussia's leadership without Austria's participation, and that it will recognize everything that Your Majesty thinks fit to do in N. Germany, provides all the essentials that Prussia demands of her. The preservation of the Kingdom of Saxony is the wish of both Austria and France. [*William I*: That besides the preservation of the Kingdom of Saxony its integrity will also be guaranteed, bears very hard on me, as Saxony was the chief instigator of the war and has come out of it unimpaired.] If, as seems likely, Austria is willing to give up her other allies in N. Germany to this end, then it seems prudent to accommodate ourselves to this, and an agreement with Saxony, which places all the military resources of the land at Your Majesty's disposal, perhaps on the basis of the conditions set up for Schleswig-Holstein on 22 Feb. 1865, would satisfy both political interest and political needs. The exclusion of Austria from the Bund, combined with the annexation of Schleswig-Holstein, Hanover, Kurhesse, Oberhesse and Nassau, and with a similar relationship of Saxony to Prussia, can be regarded as a goal so great that it could never have been envisaged at the outbreak of war. [*William I*: A result that was never envisaged, but must still be considered problematical, in view of the Congress idea.]

If this goal can be assured on this basis by a rapid conclusion of the preliminaries, then in my humble opinion it would be a political blunder to put the whole outcome in jeopardy by attempting to wrest from Austria a few more square miles of territory or a few more millions of war payments, and expose it to the risk of a prolonged war or negotiations in which foreign intervention could not be excluded. [*William I*: Agreed, but it depends on how much money or land can be acquired without risking everything in one throw.]

BE C

An outbreak of cholera in the army, and the danger that an August campaign in this climate will bring epidemics, also militate against a continuation of operations. [*William I*: Very strongly.]

If Your Majesty will give Your consent to this interpretation, I will have to seek Your Majesty's authority to present to the Landtag the necessary bills for the extension of the boundaries of the kingdom by the incorporation of Hanover, the Electorate of Hesse, Nassau, and the archducal territory of Oberhesse and Schleswig-Holstein, and thus present this whole acquisition as a *fait accompli* which, as it will have had Austria's recognition and France's agreement, cannot be contested by anyone who could endanger it. [*William I*: I am entirely in agreement.]

I hold it to be my duty to Your Majesty to present this humble report to you officially and in writing, as the present crucial decision is in my view of incalculable importance. I am very conscious of my responsibility to Your Majesty for the advice I am called upon to give, and therefore feel the necessity of confirming officially that, even if I dutifully carry out every one of Your Majesty's conditions in the negotiations, any hindering of a speedy settlement with Austria by seeking to obtain secondary advantages, will be contrary to my respectful counsel and suggestion. [*William I*: If in spite of what we apparently have the right to expect of the defeated power it is not possible to demand what the army and the country have a right to expect, namely heavy indemnities from Austria as the main enemy or territorial gain to a really visible extent, without endangering the main object (see above), then the victor will have to bite into this sour apple at the gates of Vienna and leave it to posterity to judge. Nikolsburg, 25.7.66. William.]

GW, iv, 79-81

9   Benedetti seeks Compensation for France

Bismarck to Goltz, 5 August 1866

Secret. Benedetti has just sent the following plan for a secret convention:

1. Prussia gives France the 1814 frontier.

2. Prussia persuades Bavaria and Hesse-Darmstadt to give up all territories on the left bank of the Rhine to France, stipulating indemnities to be paid *by us*.

3. Prussia relinquishes all links with Limburg and Luxemburg, and garrison rights in the latter.

As there is no mention of a quid pro quo for Prussia, this is the compensation for our annexations.

This sharply contradicts everything that the Emperor has repeatedly told you. I would never entertain the slightest hope of getting the King's consent to this, but will in any case not propose anything so extensive. I am sending you this preliminary account for your own personal information, without prejudice to a further communication in due course.

Oncken, ii, 22

10   Bismarck repels Benedetti

Bismarck to Goltz, 8 August 1866

... The Emperor justifies his demands by reference to his country and public opinion; we counter that by referring to our country and our public opinion. We cannot reconcile with the good sense, which we normally admire in him, the making of demands upon us which involve a humiliation of Prussia, and which will inevitably lead to fresh irreconcilable animosity of Prussians and Germans towards France.

I repeat the question: What is the aim and final purpose of the Emperor Napoleon with this new departure?

His Majesty the King expresses the fear that the Emperor will push it as far as a breach with Prussia; and I cannot help feeling that this fear is justified, at least in the diplomatic sphere.

I did not conceal from the ambassador that his communications would make this impression, and that at the present moment I should consider it wiser not to pursue it any further. But his instructions seem this time to be much more peremptory.

M. Benedetti did declare, 'We shall not make war for that', but he forecast lasting ill-humour on the part of the Emperor and his government, which would have a fateful influence on the whole position....

Oncken, ii, 28-32

11   Treaty of Prague, 23 August 1866

Article I. [Peace and Friendship established between Austria and Prussia henceforth and for ever.]

Article II. [The Emperor of Austria accedes to declaration of the French ambassador of 29 July 1866 respecting cession of Venice to

Italy, and gives his consent to the Union of the Lombardo-Venetian Kingdom with the Kingdom of Italy, without any other burdensome condition than the liquidation of relevant debts.]

Article III. [Prisoners of war to be set at liberty immediately.]

Article IV. His Majesty the Emperor of Austria acknowledges the dissolution of the Germanic Confederation as hitherto constituted, and gives his consent to a new organisation of Germany without the participation of the Imperial Austrian State. His Majesty likewise promises to recognize the more restricted Federal relations which His Majesty the King of Prussia will establish to the north of the line of the Main; and he declares his concurrence in the formation of an Association of the German States situated to the south of that line, whose national connexion with the North German Confederation is reserved for further arrangement between the parties, and which will have an independent international existence.

Article V. His Majesty the Emperor of Austria transfers to His Majesty the King of Prussia all the rights which he acquired by the Vienna Treaty of Peace of 30 October 1864 over the Duchies of Holstein and Schleswig, with the condition that the populations of the Northern Districts of Schleswig shall be ceded to Denmark if, by a free vote, they express a wish to be united to Denmark.

Article VI. [Existing territorial condition of Saxony to remain as before.] ...

Article XI. His Majesty the Emperor of Austria undertakes to pay to His Majesty the King of Prussia the sum of 40,000,000 Prussian thalers, to cover part of the expenses which Prussia has been put to by the War. From that sum is however to be deducted the amount of the War expenses which His Majesty the Emperor of Austria has still to demand from the Duchies of Schleswig and Holstein, according to Article XII of the aforesaid Treaty of Vienna of the 30th October, 1864, to the extent of 15,000,000 Prussian thalers, as well as a further sum of 5,000,000, as an equivalent for the free maintenance which the Prussian Army is to have in those parts of the Austrian Territories which it occupies, until the conclusion of Peace; so that there only remain 20,000,000 to be paid in ready money.

One-half of that sum is to be settled when the Ratification of the present Treaty takes place, the second half 3 weeks later at Oppeln in cash.

Article XII. [Prussian evacuation of Austrian territories to be completed in 3 weeks.]

Article XIII. [All treaties and conventions concluded between Austria and Prussia before the war to be again brought into force, where applicable; the 'Zollverein' treaty of 11 April 1865 to be revised for the further facilitation of their reciprocal traffic.] . . .

(L.S. BRENNER
(L.S.) WERTHER
Hertslet, iii, 1720-6

D

THE FRENCH PROBLEM, 1867-1870

The consolidation of Prussia's new relationship with north Germany was a complicated task, involving treaties with the smaller states, long and exhausting debates on the constitution, the drawing-up of new legal codes, and the re-negotiation of the *Zollverein* treaties. This phase of state building could in itself account for the fact that Bismarck seemed in no hurry to complete German unification by the incorporation of the four states south of the Main— Baden, Bavaria, Hesse-Darmstadt, and Württemberg—but there were other reasons for his circumspection. One was that nationalist feeling in the four states was not yet strong enough to sweep aside those particularist, Catholic, anti-Prussian elements which if challenged too roughly might turn to Austria or France for support. Another was that the governments of these states, even if they came voluntarily into the north German Confederation, would reinforce the opponents of centralization during the constitutional debates. Most important of all, perhaps, was the fact that Europe needed time to get used to the new Germany, and that if war with France—the most likely opponent— became necessary he wanted to fight her alone; undoubtedly, too, he wanted to be sure that war *was* necessary.

(a) *The Luxemburg question.* The foreign policy of Prussia during the twelve months following the Nikolsburg treaty was concerned almost entirely with Napoleon's efforts to derive some benefit from and avoid humiliation over the Prussian success. After his show of indignation over Drouyn de Lhuys's terms on 5 August 1866 (C, **10**) Bismarck temporized over further French proposals. In mid-August Napoleon proposed that France should acquire the frontiers of 1814 and Luxemburg, and should sign an offensive and defensive alliance with Prussia under which France could eventually acquire Belgium. Although objecting to the demand for the 1814 frontier, which Napoleon promptly dropped, Bismarck did not rule out the rest of the plan, of which Benedetti was unwise enough to give him a written version on 29 August. After this, during the winter of 1866-7, Bismarck was always too ill or too busy to discuss the matter much further, although he appeared amenable over French plans to secure Luxemburg.

Frenchmen were justified in some apprehension over the security of their frontiers as they watched the increase of German power. Napoleon faced the contradiction that had confused his Italian policy: his role as the champion of nationalism conflicted with his imperial duty to prevent the power balance being tilted against his country. Furthermore, his personal aspiration to a preponderant voice in international arrangements made it humiliating for him to be ignored: he would like it to appear that he had personally dictated the limits of Prussian advance. The cession of Venice and the halting of Prussia on the Main line could be regarded as successes for his diplomacy, and he boasted to the French parliament on 14 February 1867 that without moving a single regiment he had halted the victorious Prussians at the gates of Vienna in July 1866.

But French opinion was uneasy, although unwarlike; Napoleon's critics blamed him for lack of decisive leadership, and Thiers remarked that war would be the only mistake which the Empire had not yet made. In the important debate in the French parliament on 14-18 March 1867 the opposition were unconvinced by the official view that as a threefold division of Germany had replaced the German Confederation, France's position was improved. The publication on 19 March 1867 of details of three Prussian defensive treaties of August 1866 with Baden, Bavaria, and Württemberg was a further sickening blow to Napoleon's prestige, as Bismarck was evidently aware.

Bismarck found it useful to whip up the appearance of a crisis with France at this point when the crucial debates in the constituent Reichstag were taking place, but he was probably not seeking war. He had acquiesced rather tepidly in the plans of the importunate French in Luxemburg, providing that they staged the affair neatly. Luxemburg was joined to Holland by a personal union; it had been (under protest) a member of the German Confederation since 1839 and had a Prussian garrison in its fortress, but the link with the Confederation was now dissolved and the population was pro-French. King William III of Holland agreed on 19 March 1867 to sell the duchy to France. But Bismarck then complained that the French had overdone the stage-managed demonstrations in their favour in Luxemburg (which he had previously condoned). He himself adroitly stage-managed an interpellation on the subject by the National-Liberal leader Bennigsen, on 1 April; although he replied in cautious terms it was made clear to Napoleon that Prussia could not now support the cession because German public feeling against it was aroused. On 3 April Bismarck warned the Dutch that war could hardly be avoided if the sale went through. On 5 April the King of Holland dropped the plan. Finally, with a not very good grace, Bismarck accepted the compromise of the London conference (7-11 May 1867) by which the duchy was neutralized and the Prussian troops withdrawn (3).

(b) *The European alignment, 1867-9.* Was Bismarck using the Luxemburg crisis merely for internal effect? He was a vindictive and competitive man who repeatedly humiliated domestic and foreign opponents throughout his career, and he may well have enjoyed putting Napoleon in his place. In the Luxemburg treaty he insisted on making the withdrawal of the Prussian garrison dependent on the general guarantee of the signatory powers of the neutrality of the state, which deprived Napoleon of any appearance of advantage, whereas a little harmless political success for him might have greatly improved the general prospect of peace. It has been argued that Bismarck was really trying in April to provoke France into a declaration of war, hoping presumably to generate a wave of national German enthusiasm which would sweep aside all obstacles to unification. But at the same time (on 30 March) he had revealed to Goltz his interest in a bargain whereby France would take Luxemburg and agree in return to release Prussia from her undertaking to divide Schleswig according to nationalities. It has also been argued that the crisis marks his transition from a Prussian to a Germanic outlook on foreign affairs. This is true in so far as the Luxemburg crisis was the first to face the new North German Confederation; but a doubtful assertion if it is meant to suggest that he was moved by some newly found nationalist sentiment.[1] The most likely explanation seems to be that Bismarck found an atmosphere of crisis with France at this time more profitable than a bargain, but did not desire war because the international political situation (as distinct from the military) was by no means favourable.

On 3 April Stanley, the British foreign secretary, had decisively rejected Bismarck's proposal of an Anglo-Prussian alliance to defend Belgium (1). The tsar, increasingly worried by fresh disturbances in Turkey, was more interested in Crete than in Luxemburg, and having failed to reach agreement with either France or Austria over the eastern question was in no mood to welcome a major crisis in the west. Since the end of 1866 Bismarck had been sounding Vienna as to the possibility of closer Austro-Prussian relations, a course favoured by Prince Hohenlohe, chief minister of Bavaria, as the best antidote to a Franco-Austrian alliance. Count Beust, a Saxon and a declared enemy of Bismarck, who became Austrian foreign minister in place of Mensdorff in October 1866 and minister president in February 1867, was quite unresponsive. He was shocked by the announcement of Bismarck's secret treaties with the three south German states, which he later described as a masterpiece of disloyal negotiation.[2] In mid-April 1967 Bismarck welcomed Hohenlohe's agent, Baron Tauffkirchen, who brought plans for closer links between Bavaria, Prussia, and Austria; Bismarck proposed an alliance linking all the German states and the possible addition of Russia. But when Tauffkirchen took these proposals to Vienna, Beust made it clear that he saw little advantage in the arrangement for Austria (2). Gorchakov, told of the plan, dismissed the idea of a revival of the Holy Alliance in view of Austro-Russian rivalry in the Balkans.

To this unsympathetic reaction of foreign governments had to be added the absence of any wave of irresistible nationalist fervour in the south. In Dr. Pflanze's words, 'the Luxemburg crisis had failed to provide the needed steam for the engine of Bismarck's German policy.'[3] During the next three years

[1] Erich Eyck, *Bismarck* (Erlenbach-Zurich, 1943), ii, 366-7; Walter Bussmann, *Das Zeitalter Bismarcks* (Konstanz, 1956), p. 108.

[2] Graf von Beust, *Aus Drei Viertel-Jahrhunderten* (Stuttgart, 1887), ii, 117.

[3] Pflanze, p. 390.

Bismarck made without success a number of moves in the hope of generating sufficient support for unity. The most important of these was the setting up of a 'Zollparlament', with delegates from all German states; but the majority of the deputies from the four southern states were pledged to limit the discussions to strictly commercial problems. Adopting a very reserved attitude towards the eastern question, which was the main preoccupation of the remaining powers in 1868 and 1869, he had in mind all the time the possibility of a French war, provoked in some way or other by the Prussian challenge to French prestige or security. The army was ready for action. If Bismarck did not respond to von Moltke's suggestion of a preventive war it was not because of moral scruple but because of the political inexpediency of such brash action.

The Russo-German agreement of March 1868, a vital factor in Bismarck's success in 1870, was a highly successful result of this more economical diplomacy. France and Austria, while ever anxious to resist and if possible diminish Prussia's growing power in central Europe, were aware that their battered political images might be more easily restored by successes in Turkey. A meeting between Napoleon and Franz Joseph at Salzburg in August 1867 produced plans for joint action, but no written commitments. They could count on British support in Constantinople, although not in central Europe. It looked as if Beust was aiming at a forward policy in the Balkans with a revival of the Crimean alignment, and possible gains in Bosnia and the Hercegovina.

In considerable alarm, the tsar spoke to King William early in February 1868 of the need for a Russo-Prussian alliance which would operate *pari passu* against Austria and France. The Prussian reply was friendly and non-committal. In March the tsar tried again. On 20 March Oubril brought a Russian offer to place 100,000 men on the Austrian frontier to keep Austria quiet in the event of a Franco-Prussian war, on the understanding that if Russia were threatened by Austria, Prussia would similarly keep France quiet. Bismarck welcomed the idea of reciprocal support on these lines, but evaded any written agreement on the ground that it might be provocative when it became known and because the self-interest of the two powers in any case made it unnecessary. He thus adroitly secured Russian protection of his Austrian flank in the event of a French war, without undertaking to oppose Austrian plans in Bosnia or elsewhere (4). Gorchakov accepted this, although he had hoped for more. A French mission which visited St. Petersburg in October 1869 failed to weaken the Russo-Prussian alignment.

(c) *Origins of 1870 war: the Hohenzollern candidature*. Three problems face the historian at this point. Did Bismarck regard an early war with France as essential to the success of his German policy? Did France, convinced of the inevitability of war, force it on? Did Bismarck, ingeniously provocative, produce this conviction? In each case there is some conflict of evidence, but on balance an affirmative answer.

It is certainly true that south German opposition to the completion of unity had not diminished by the beginning of 1870, and that a war with France was the one likely means of rapidly swinging over popular feeling in the four states.

But Bismarck can be quoted as an opponent of attempts to force the pace. He wrote to Baron von Werthern, Prussian minister in Munich, on 26 February 1869, to deprecate any such 'arbitrary interference in the course of history.'[4] A year later he told Moritz Busch that German unity might take ten years to achieve. And yet these and similar pacific utterances do not square with others, which included reference to the French veto on German unification as an inevitable cause of early war. He was opposed, it would seem, to war against the southern states but not against France. He knew that Napoleon might be driven to fight by the war party, although he was hopeful for a time that the formation of a liberal government under Émile Ollivier at the end of 1869 might ensure peace (that is, acquiescence in German developments). With this there went a series of moves undoubtedly aimed at whipping up national German feeling, probably with an eye to the forthcoming Reichstag elections and the securing of the military budget. One of these plans, much discussed between January and March 1870, was for proclaiming King William emperor (the 'Kaiser project').

These developments again demonstrate Bismarck's ability to pursue alternative lines of policy until the time for advantageous choice. The Hohenzollern candidature, which provided the immediate cause of war in July 1870, also had alternative possibilities: if successful it would (a) help the Kaiser project by enhancing Hohenzollern prestige; (b) make France the aggressor if the event goaded her into a declaration of war; (c) divide French forces and inflict another diplomatic humiliation on Napoleon if he acquiesced. The ultimate secrets of the German foreign office with regard to the candidature have now been revealed in Dr. Bonnin's publication.[5] A Spanish emissary, Salazar y Mazarredo, probably with Bismarck's approval, offered Prince Leopold of Hohenzollern the Spanish throne, which had been vacant since 1868, in September 1869; it was refused, but the offer was repeated by General Prim, the Spanish prime minister, in February 1870. Although Bismarck on 16 July 1870 denied to the Reichstag any official cognizance of the offer before 3 July (9) he had in fact thrown his full weight on the side of acceptance in March, in spite of the objections of King William, as head of the Hohenzollern family. Bismarck's arguments, as set out in an important memorandum of 9 March, covered every eventuality except the most obvious one, namely that France would be driven to make war.[6] Even without this, William made incisive objections in his marginal comments on the memorandum, and he maintained his refusal in spite of weighty arguments from his advisers at a meeting on 15 March (5). Nevertheless, Bismarck continued through his agents, Lothar Bucher and Major von Versen, to encourage Prim to persist and Prince Leopold to accept, and the prince's agreement was finally secured on 19 June, subject to the king's permission (6). This was grudgingly given on 21 June.

[4] Pflanze, pp. 433-4.
[5] Georges Bonnin, *Bismarck and the Hohenzollern Candidature for the Spanish Throne* (London, 1957).   [6] Bonnin, pp. 68-73.

The French reaction to the candidature led to war, but not on lines that Bismarck could have anticipated. The intention had been to present Napoleon and the world with a *fait accompli*, in the form of a speedy election of the prince by the Spanish Cortes; but before this could happen there was a misunderstanding and the Cortes was prorogued on 23 June until the following November. The news began to leak, and Prim announced the candidature to the French ambassador on 3 July. Gramont, the French foreign minister, at once telegraphed an enquiry to Berlin as to its knowledge of 'this intrigue', and was told at the foreign office that the Prussian government knew nothing about it. On 4 July the inspired French press spoke indignantly of the affair, and on the 6th Gramont made a chauvinistic speech to the French chamber. Benedetti was instructed to ask King William to secure Leopold's renunciation of his candidacy. The king, who wanted to keep the peace and also his own dignity, did not conceal from Benedetti his previous acceptance of the candidacy, but indicated that, at least as a matter of form, a renunciation must come from the prince himself. The prince's father did announce the renunciation on 12 July, although only after four days of uncertainty which much increased the tension in Paris.

If only Gramont had been content with this diplomatic success, which Bismarck regarded as a second Olmütz for Prussia, war might still have been avoided. But various forms of a statement to be demanded from King William were discussed in Paris. Benedetti later argued that Gramont exceeded his instructions from Napoleon when he telegraphed to Benedetti on the evening of the 12th to ask for an assurance that the king would not authorize a renewal of the candidature (7). The king's refusal on the 13th to give the pledge demanded and his decision not to receive Benedetti a second time that day formed the subject of a telegram to Bismarck from Abeken, a foreign office official accompanying the king (11,i). Shortened, this became the famous 'Ems telegram' (11,ii). It has recently been shown[7] that Bismarck's gleeful account of this episode in his memoirs, written in the 1890s, considerably oversimplifies the story, and a careful study of the French press suggests that the publication of the telegram had little to do with the decision of Napoleon and his close advisers late on 14 July to mobilize the French army.[8] Ollivier justified his policy to the *Corps Législatif* on more general grounds on the 15th, and the declaration of war followed.

Lord Lyons, the British ambassador, saw the real cause of the war in the French conviction that 'they must have it out with Prussia sooner or later' and that a better chance was not likely to recur. Bismarck's consistent and much publicized evasion of all concessions to the French interests and point of view since 1866 built up French animosity in proportion as it furthered German

[7] By W. L. Langer in an essay, 'Bismarck as a Dramatist' (*Studies in Diplomatic History and Historiography*, ed. A. O. Sarkissian (1961), pp. 199-216).

[8] E. M. Carroll, *French Public Opinion and Foreign Affairs, 1870-1914* (New York, 1931), pp. 31-5.

nationalist fervour. But Bismarck played this dangerous political game with vastly greater skill than Napoleon and his men. While Gramont was in error in counting on Austrian support, Bismarck could rely on his unwritten understanding with Russia (10). By forcing on the war the French put themselves in the wrong in the eyes of influential neutrals. Above all, Bismarck was right, Napoleon tragically wrong, in their estimates of the relative efficiency of the Prussian and French armies.

1 Stanley rejects an Anglo-Prussian Alliance

Stanley to Cowley, draft despatch, 3 April 1867

[Count Bernstorff speaks to Lord Stanley about the position of Belgium in the event of a Franco-Prussian war over Luxemburg.] He did not see how a war could be avoided, and in the event of its taking place, and of France obtaining any success, the position of Belgium would become exceedingly precarious. He was anxious therefore to know whether, in the event of war being forced on Prussia by France, Her Majesty's Government would take part in it and to what extent they would give their cooperation to Prussia?

I said that was a question which I could answer without hesitation. England was on the most friendly terms with both France and Prussia; with the causes of their quarrel, if unfortunately a quarrel were to break out, she had absolutely nothing to do and I felt sure that no minister, whatever his political connexion or tendency might be, would venture to propose to Parliament, nor would public opinion sanction, an armed interference on either side.

[England was pledged to assist in maintaining Belgian independence.] But there was a wide distinction between taking up arms in case of necessity for the protection of Belgium, in fulfilment of promises solemnly and repeatedly given, and joining in a war between France and Germany, in which no English interest was involved and with regard to which we stood absolutely free and unpledged. . . .

RA I 71/31: Mosse, p. 264

2 Beust rejects an Austro-Prussian Alliance

Beust to Count Wimpffen, 19 April 1867

. . . Count Tauffkirchen on his visit here conducted himself not only as the representative of his government, but also as the bearer of important proposals from Prussia. He gave as the reason for his appearance in Berlin the wish of Prince Hohenlohe to clarify the eventualities of the Luxemburg question, to preserve the interests of peace in association with Prussia, and with this in view to make an especial effort to see whether Bavaria could succeed in bringing about a rapprochement between Austria and Prussia. His success with Bismarck was of great importance. He had been put in the position of advocating the conclusion of an alliance between the two powers, an alliance which would extend to all German states. The preservation of peace would be assured by such a confederation. They did not fail to recognize in Berlin that Austria was justified in asking compensation for the obligations it would be undertaking, they would, however, be prepared to go as far as possible in meeting them.

What Count Tauffkirchen added on this point was, however, unfortunately not the most lucid part of his disclosures.

He spoke of a guarantee of our *German* possessions. He let it be understood that for our *non-German* provinces there could also *temporarily* be offered adequate security against possible dangers. He mentioned Russia as the third member of the group and expressed it as his opinion that a renewal of the three power alliance would produce this security. He finally indicated—as had been done earlier in Munich —that a treaty of friendship between Prussia and Austria would make it possible for the south German states to assert a greater measure of independence, and that an international alliance of Austria with the north German and south German confederations could finally lead to close ties by treaty, which could with advantage to both to Austria and the German nation replace the earlier confederation of states.

[In reply, Beust finds little advantage in the proposals for Austria.] 'But now imagine the possible consequences of war. You will admit that it would be no happy fate to suffer a joint defeat with Prussia, and to have to submit to the laws of the conqueror on the Rhine, beneath the Alps and on the Adriatic. But dismissing this as an improbability, and assuming France is beaten—can we let it come to the point when they will press the Prague instrument of peace into our hands and thank us for its successful defence? Far be it from me to awaken memories of our joint victory over Denmark, but you will understand that in the light of that most favourable eventuality, we must take steps *beforehand* to guard against possible threats to our security.' . . .

Count Tauffkirchen . . . merely expressed his regret that he must assume from my words that Austria would *reject* the proposals he had brought from Berlin. . . .

Graf von Beust, *Aus Drei Viertel-Jahrhunderten* (Stuttgart, 1887), ii, 119-23

3 The Luxemburg and Limburg Treaty, 11 May 1867

[Signed by Great Britain, Austria, Belgium, France, Italy, the Netherlands, Prussia, and Russia at London]

Article I. His Majesty the King of the Netherlands, Grand Duke of Luxemburg, maintains the ties which attach the said Grand Duchy to the House of Orange-Nassau. . . .

Article II. The Grand Duchy of Luxemburg, within the Limits determined by the Act annexed to the Treaties of the 19th April, 1839, under the Guarantee of the Courts of Great Britain, Austria, France, Prussia, and Russia, shall henceforth form a perpetually Neutral State.

It shall be bound to observe the same Neutrality towards all other States.

The High Contracting Parties engage to respect the principle of Neutrality stipulated by the present Article.

That principle is and remains placed under the sanction of the collective Guarantee of the Powers signing Parties to the present Treaty, with the exception of Belgium, which is itself a Neutral State.

Article III. The Grand Duchy of Luxemburg being Neutralized, according to the terms of the preceding Article, the maintenance or establishment of Fortresses upon its Territory becomes without necessity as well as without object.

In consequence, it is agreed by common consent that the City of Luxemburg, considered in time past, in a military point of view, as a Federal Fortress, shall cease to be a fortified city.

His Majesty the King Grand Duke reserves to himself to maintain in that city the number of troops necessary to provide in it for the maintenance of good order.

Article IV. In conformity with the stipulations contained in Articles II and III, His Majesty the King of Prussia declares that his troops actually in garrison in the Fortress of Luxemburg shall receive orders to proceed to the Evacuation of that place immediately after the exchange of the Ratifications of the present Treaty. . . .

Article V. His Majesty the King Grand Duke . . . engages, on his part, to take the necessary measures for converting the said Fortress into an open city by means of a demolition which His Majesty shall deem sufficient. . . . [Fortifications not to be restored.]

Article VI. [The dissolution of the Germanic Confederation has produced the dissolution of the ties which united the Duchy of Limburg to the Confederation; the Duchy will continue to form an integral part of the Kingdom of the Netherlands.]

Hertslet, iii, 1803-5

4 Russo-Prussian Agreement of March 1868

Bismarck to Reusz (St. Petersburg), no. 114 secret, 22 March 1868

[Oubril has sought interview with Bismarck on 20 March.] . . . M. d'Oubril was instructed to show me an extract from a Paris despatch in which France's intentions were discussed and the conviction voiced that France would wait until Austria had sufficiently recovered her strength and was adequately rearmed, but would then seek an occasion for war with Prussia—an opinion which, in my view, judging from the prevailing mood in Paris and Vienna, is not at all improbable. To meet this eventuality M. d'Oubril—as H.M. the Emperor had already indicated personally to Your Excellency and Colonel v. Schweinitz—suggested the stationing of 100,000 troops on the Austrian frontier, to keep Austria in check and prevent her from taking an active part in the war, with the definite proviso that if Russia were threatened, Prussia would do the same.

My answer to the Imperial Ambassador was as follows: I begged him to judge the genuineness of our convictions from the fact that I needed no reflection before stating my own agreement and the certainty of H.M. the King's concurrence with this proposal; I was completely and firmly convinced that there was no other policy open to Prussia, and I had often had occasion to ascertain the views of H.M. the King on such eventualities and could be sure that H.M. would completely approve of this attitude, and would recognize in the proposed mutual action the expression of a natural and inevitable policy on the part of the two powers. I requested M. d'Oubril to report the immediate and unhesitating declaration in St. Petersburg, and I likewise request Your Excellency to support it by your own attitude.

. . . It is natural that at his age and after the brilliant successes of the last few years, the fruits of which he would like to see ripen in peace, His Majesty is peaceably inclined and would like to avoid the hazards of a fresh war; and he fears that the conclusion of a treaty of alliance to meet the case of war could, in fact, lead to such a war, because the alliance could not remain secret, and knowledge of it would prompt the formation of counter alliances on the other side, which would necessarily raise the tension step by step, until at last war resulted, without anyone w:nting it. Experience shows that such a preoccupation is not unjustified, also that the maintenance of secrecy about specific written documents is very difficult. . . .

I told M. d'Oubril in our last conversation that we thought we were equal to a war against France *alone* and would have no need to spread the war, if Russia would only protect our rear against Austria. We assumed that Russia's attitude would be the same, if she were involved in a war with Austria and we were to guarantee her against support of Austria by France. But as soon as one of us, Prussia or Russia, should be attacked by a coalition of two powers, common interest would compel either power to come to the aid of the other. . . .

APP, ix, 801-3

5   A Prussian Crown Council

Prince Karl Anton to Prince Charles of Rumania, 20 March 1870

I have been occupied here for the last fortnight with very important family affairs: nothing less than acceptance or refusal of the Spanish throne for Leopold which, under the seal of a European state secret it is true, has been officially offered by the Spanish government.

The question is preoccupying Berlin. Bismarck would like acceptance for dynastic and political reasons, but the King only if Leopold *willingly* responds to the call. On the 15th there was a very interesting and important council presided over by the King, at which the Crown Prince, we two, Bismarck, Roon, Moltke, Schleinitz, Thile and

Delbrück were present. The unanimous resolution of the councillors was for acceptance, as a Prussian patriotic duty. For many reasons, and after a hard tussle, Leopold refused. But as now in Spain they would like above all a Catholic Hohenzoller, I proposed Fritz, supposing he would accept, of course. At the moment he is between Nizza and Paris, and the telegraph has not been able to reach him or discover his whereabouts. This in short is the position, and I hope that he will allow himself to be nominated for it.

... Don Salazar, whom you saw at Weinburg, had come with a communication from Prim to Berlin; he has now gone back, because it might have become known that a Spanish representative was here, having frequent conversations with Bismarck....

Aus dem Leben König Karls von
Rumänien (Stuttgart, 1894), ii, 72

6   The Hohenzollern Princes discuss Tactics

From Major von Versen's diary, 19 June 1870

... The Hereditary Prince said that with a heavy heart but with the consciousness of acting in the interest of the State he asked the King's permission to accept. The letter was worded in such a way that the Hereditary Prince intimated that he was making a sacrifice for the renown of the family and the weal of the Fatherland; but it was at the same time phrased so that the King only needed to reply: 'no objection'. The Hereditary Prince repeated what he had said to me already several times, namely, that 'he had to say this because he was not acting either from self-interest or on any special impulse, and he did not want to appear as a "climber" '. Bucher induced Prince Karl Anton to accompany this letter of the Hereditary Prince's with one of his own to the King in which he said: 'Only on grounds of Family Law did his son thus apply for permission and he trusted the King would have no objections to make.' The question now arose who was to go to the King. Bucher looked at me as if I should be the one. I said the best thing would be for Herr Bucher to go, for the King is furious that I am not at Posen. Then there came various scruples on Prince Karl Anton's part. What would France say about it? Would it not give rise to complications? I said: 'Bismarck says that is just what he is looking for.'

Karl Anton: Yes, Count Bismarck may want it, but is it really in the interests of the State?

Myself: Yes, Bismarck's interests and those of the State are the same thing.

Bucher: I can only say what Bismarck has often said to me: if in these last years Napoleon had wanted war he could have found plenty of grounds for it. . . .

Bonnin, pp. 277-8

7 Gramont seeks Satisfaction

[M. de Gramont wrote later that on 12 July he] 'submitted to [the Prussian ambassador, Baron von Werther's] appreciation whether the proper mode to employ would not be a letter from the King to the Emperor. . . . Baron von Werther on his part, without formally agreeing to this suggestion, did not oppose its discussion, as his despatch shows. . .'.

During the interview [between Napoleon III and Gramont] at Saint Cloud, the proposal I [Benedetti] was instructed to make was substituted for the one which had been suggested to the Prussian Ambassadors. The difference was considerable: I had to ask the King neither for a letter nor the justification of his previous conduct; I had merely to solicit a verbal declaration guaranteeing us against the repetition of a candidature we could not submit to.

But what more than abundantly proves that the Emperor never for a moment agreed to M. de Gramont's suggestion is that, during the evening [of 12 July], shortly after their interview, he thought it necessary, in order to distinctly express his way of thinking, to send [Gramont] the letter from which I have already quoted, and which I think it well to give in its entirety:

'Thinking over our conversations of today and reading Prince Anthony's telegram again, I see we must confine ourselves to giving additional emphasis to the despatch you have of course sent to Benedetti, by laying stress on the following points:

'1. We are dealing with Prussia and not with Spain.

'2. The telegram sent by Prince Anthony to Prim is a non-official document for us which nobody has been instructed, lawfully, to communicate to us.

'3. Prince Leopold consented to be a candidate for the throne of Spain, and it is his father who withdraws the candidature.

'4. It is therefore necessary that Benedetti should insist, as he has been instructed to do, upon having a reply by which the King would undertake, for the future, not to permit Prince Leopold, who has made no promise, to follow his brother's example and start, one fine day, for Spain.

'5. So long as we have not received an official communication from Ems, we are not presumed to have received an answer to our lawful demands.

'6. It is therefore impossible to make a communication to the Chambers before being better informed.'

Count Benedetti, Studies in Diplomacy (London, 1896), pp. 301, 304–6

8 The Ems Telegram

(i) *H. Abeken to Bismarck, telegram, 13 July 1870, 3.30 p.m.*

His Majesty the King writes to me: 'Count Benedetti caught me on the Promenade and importunately requested me to authorize him to send a telegram at once saying I bound myself not to consent to the Hohenzollern candidature should they recur to it at any future time; this I declined, and rather sternly at last. One cannot enter *à tout jamais* into such an engagement. I, of course, told him that I had no news, but as he got his from Paris and Madrid sooner than I did, he must understand that my Government was taking no part in the matter.'

Since then his Majesty has received a letter from Prince Karl Anton. His Majesty had informed Count Benedetti that he was expecting news from the Prince, but, having regard to the above unreasonable demand, his Majesty resolved, on the advice of Count Eulenburg and myself, not to receive Count Benedetti again, but merely to send him a message by an adjutant to the effect that his Majesty had now received from the Prince the confirmation of the news which Benedetti had already received from Paris, and that his Majesty had nothing further to say to the Ambassador. His Majesty leaves it to the decision of your Excellency whether this new demand of Benedetti and our

refusal to comply therewith should not be forthwith communicated
to our Ambassadors and to the Press.

> C. E. Barrett-Lennard and M. W.
> Hoper, *Bismarck's Pen* (London,
> 1911), p. 253

(ii) *Bismarck's revised version of the Ems telegram*

After the news of the renunciation of the Prince of Hohenzollern had
been officially communicated by the Spanish Government to the
French Government, the French Ambassador in Ems nevertheless
demanded that his Majesty should authorize him to telegraph to Paris,
that his Majesty pledged himself for all future time never again to give
his consent to the Hohenzollern resuming the candidature. His Majesty
has thereupon declined to receive the Ambassador again and has informed him through the adjutant that he has nothing further to communicate to the Ambassador.

> *Bismarck's Pen*, p. 254

9   The Hohenzollern Candidature: Bismarck's Disclaimer

Bismarck, speech in Bundesrat, 16 July 1870

. . . The events which have led Europe in the course of the last fortnight from a state of calm not experienced for years to the outbreak
of a great war have taken place so openly, that an account of the
genesis of the present situation can be nothing more than a recital of
known facts.

It is known from the communications which the President of the
Spanish ministerial council made on the 11th of last month in the
constituent Cortes, from the circular despatch of the Spanish Foreign
Minister on 7 inst., published in the press, and from a declaration which
M. Salazar y Mazarredo had printed in Madrid on 8 inst., that the
Spanish government had been negotiating for months with His
Highness the Hereditary Prince Leopold of Hohenzollern to accept the
Spanish throne, that these negotiations entrusted to M. Salazar were
carried through in direct consultation with the prince and his father,
without the participation or intervention of any other government,
and that His Highness finally decided to accept the nomination. His

Majesty the King of Prussia, who was informed of this, did not think fit to oppose the decision of an adult prince, made after mature consideration and in agreement with his father.

The foreign office of the North German Bund, and the government of H.M. the King of Prussia had had no knowledge of these proceedings. They only learned from the Havas telegram sent from Paris on 3 inst, that the Spanish ministry had decided to offer the crown to the prince....

GW, 11, 129-30

10 Reactions in Vienna to Prussia's Victory

[General von Schweinitz, Prussian ambassador in Vienna since December 1869, writes:] Napoleon had hardly been brought to safety in Wilhelmshöhe [after Sedan, 1 September 1870] before the press campaign was started in Berlin against Count Beust; the *Spenersche Zeitung*, which had prestige because it was said that it was the only one King William read, published in a prominent position a furious diatribe against the man whom the Emperor Franz Joseph in an evil moment had chosen to be his adviser. This time I was really beside myself; I saw my carefully constructed edifice, based it is true on the fictitious love of peace and German outlook of Beust, shattered by one rude blow, and at the same time the man himself strengthened in his place beside the Emperor. Those who knew the latter could not but realize that Bismarck's attack of 1866 on the enemy would necessarily have that effect. I on the other hand took the view that it would be useful, even necessary, to keep Beust in office as long as the war lasted, because he alone was clever and skilful enough to oppose the plans of the war party. But that this in itself would make him unpopular and after a brilliant peace for us he would disappear from the scene as an opponent overcome by Bismarck in every sphere. I was therefore jolted somewhat out of the calm which I had preserved hitherto in moments of serious crisis and telegraphed *ab irato* to Bismarck: 'If the intention of today's article in the *Spenersche Zeitung* was to restore Count Beust's lost popularity and to strengthen his position again, then it has achieved its goal.' This brought a not undeserved reproof; the electric wire flashed back: it was not customary in the foreign service for representatives to use sarcasm in their reports. The article in the *Spenersche Zeitung* was however immediately flatly contradicted officially, and that was the main thing for me. Already on 5 September

I had received a forceful telegram from headquarters concerning Count Beust; Count Bismarck asked me why I had contested the undoubted truth that Beust was a hindrance to our rapprochement with Austria. I answered, because Beust's *present* likely successor could be more dangerous than he himself; it could be just an ultramontanist, a francophile Magyar or a biased adherent of Russia. . . .

On 14 November I had a telegram from Count Bismarck; Russia's step [repudiating the convention of 30 March 1856 concerning the Black Sea] was not discussed with us, we were only informed a little earlier than the other powers. Count Andrássy came to dinner alone, in order to discuss the Russian note with me; he stayed four hours. . . . I tell him quite openly that as soon as we are forced to choose between Russia and Austria-Hungary, we shall have to decide on the former; nor do I conceal from him the reasons, of which the first is the reliability of the Emperor Alexander II. The Count considers this reason more important than all others, for he is firmly convinced that we are not without danger from Russia; nor do I deny this, as far as the future is concerned. The Hungarian minister-president was very perturbed over the unilateral alteration of the Paris treaties by Russia; he was glad to hear that we had known nothing about it; I did not conceal from him that we were not minded to oppose it, and he was able to say the same for himself.

Schweinitz, i, 274-5, 282

11 The Reaction of an Englishman to France's Defeat

Sir Robert Morier (Darmstadt) to Lady Derby, letter, 5 January 1871

. . . That this trial of strength should have resulted in the consolidation of Germany, *i.e.* in the fulfilment of a natural law (which until fulfilled would have necessarily kept Europe in a state of fever and turmoil) and in the rooting up, once for all, of the pretension of France to a privileged and exceptional position in Europe, seems to me so desirable an event that I confess myself totally incapable from the political point of view to understand any one in his senses wishing the result to have been otherwise. It seems to me, in order to establish the positive proof of the beneficence of this result, sufficient to consider for one moment what would have been the result of French victory: the re-establishment of the divisions and impotence of Germany from which every European war for the last three centuries has arisen, and a new lease of Napoleonism, *i.e.* the establishment thenceforth on a tolerable firm basis by Napoléon le Petit of the ideas of Napoléon le Grand.

I come back, therefore, to the thesis from which I started, that, *putting the emotional aspect of the war aside*, I must continue to declare that I consider its political results as beneficial. . . .

*Memoirs and Letters of Sir Robert
Morier*, ii, 219

E

FRANCE AND THE CATHOLIC
QUESTION, 1871-1875

With the defeat of France, Bismarck was in a position to realize the political objectives which he had pursued since the eighteen-fifties. Prussia had been established as the dominant power in a German state as extensive as he wished to make it; the opposition of Austria, France, and the particularist German governments had been overcome; his own position was assured. The constitution of 1867 was adopted with little alteration on 16 April 1871 as that of the new German Empire, which had been proclaimed in the Hall of Mirrors at Versailles on 18 January 1871. It now included the four southern states of Baden, Bavaria, Hesse, and Württemberg. For reasons both of temperament and expediency Bismarck was content henceforth to maintain and exploit this splendid position, and not to extend it. Germany was a 'satiated' state.

(a) *France: peace settlement and indemnity.* Accordingly the aim of his foreign, and also his domestic, policy during the next five years was consolidation, while he warily defended the new empire against its diverse enemies, imagined or real. French animosity was real. To the humiliation of defeat had been added onerous peace terms. Napoleon III had surrendered with a large part of his army at Sedan on 2 September 1870; the efforts of the government of National Defence had ended with the bombardment of Paris by the Germans and the conclusion of an armistice at Versailles on 28 January 1871. By an additional convention of 15 February the unconquered fortress of Belfort was surrendered. The wisdom of Bismarck's decisions in the subsequent peace negotiations has generally been denied, just as the leniency of his settlement with Austria in 1866 has often been exaggerated. It is important to remember that at the time his authority was under continued challenge from the Prussian general staff; it was only after the direct intervention of King William in January 1871 that he and not von Moltke was entrusted with the armistice and peace negotiations. But Bismarck had encouraged the popular demand for Alsace and Lorraine by means of inspired articles in the German press since August 1870, so we cannot assume that he was satisfying the demand of the soldiers for a defensible frontier against his will. He seems to have accepted the argument that as future Franco-German antagonism was inevitable Germany might as well take some real military advantage from her victory.

In the preliminary peace negotiations with Thiers in February 1871 Bismarck demanded the cession of Alsace and eastern Lorraine with the fortresses of Metz and Belfort and an indemnity of six milliards of francs. After much striving by Thiers, Bismarck finally reduced the indemnity to five milliards, and offered to leave Belfort to France if in return Prussian troops could parade through Paris. Thiers promptly accepted this bargain. A preliminary peace treaty was signed on 26 February. The definitive peace treaty, signed on 10 May 1871, followed the main lines of the preliminary treaty, with some modifications of the boundaries previously laid down (1). Apart from the territorial cession the indemnity arrangements (*Article VII*) were the most significant part of the settlement. France was to pay the first two milliards on certain fixed dates up to 1 May 1872, and the last three milliards on 2 March 1874. Until the payment was completed, German troops would continue to occupy six French departments and the fortress of Belfort. Thus if France preferred to fight rather than complete the payments, Germany would be well placed to strike back; if France delayed payment without fighting, Germany would be well poised to coerce her. As Bismarck showed in a remarkably blunt talk with the French *chargé* in August 1871 he assumed that a further war was inevitable, and feared that it would come sooner rather than later. The French for their part feared, or professed to fear, an early German preventive attack (5).

The French were irreconcilable, but the government had no intention of launching an early war. It was determined to hasten the ending of the occupation by completing the indemnity payments as soon as possible. Bismarck was not opposed to this. Although his views fluctuated, he preferred on balance a moderate republican government in France headed by Thiers to a monarchical alternative which would more easily, as he thought, find allies, and would more easily unite the country. After this he preferred a Napoleonic restoration to the return of the Bourbons.[1] In the course of these transactions Bismarck's distrust of Count von Arnim, German ambassador to Paris since December 1871, grew; although strengthened by Bismarck's belief in Arnim's intrigues at court and ambition to replace him it was based on a genuine difference of opinion about France. Arnim favoured a monarchical restoration; he believed that republicanism would promote French unity and on 3 October he suggested the overthrow of Thiers and a disruptive intervention in French politics (3,i). Bismarck rejected and thoroughly disapproved this programme (3,ii). Conventions of 12 October 1871, 29 June 1872, and 15 March 1873 regulated the stages of payment and evacuation and allowed France to hasten the completion of the instalments, so that the last German troops left France on 15 September 1873. Nevertheless, when MacMahon replaced Thiers in May 1873 Bismarck was convinced of Arnim's complicity in this revolution, and refused to be mollified by Arnim's reassuring words to the Emperor (8).

(b) *The Three Emperors' League, 1872-3.* If England remained isolationist, and France remained isolated, the three empires, Russia, Austria, and Germany,

[1] Bert Böhmer, *Frankreich Zwischen Republik und Monarchie in der Bismarckzeit* (Kullmünz, 1966), pp. 73-5 on Bismarck's preference for Bonapartism, 1867-75.

would, if united, dominate Europe. Bismarck could not forget, however, that Austro-Russian tension over the Balkans had thrown Russia onto his side in 1868, and had brought Austria and France together. A continuance of Austro-Russian tension might again give France an ally, and perhaps lead to a revival of the 'Crimean' grouping of 1856; and Beust in Vienna was still considered to be Bismarck's enemy (D,10). The traditional view is that Bismarck formed the triple grouping in order to conjure away these difficulties. The fact is, however, that the initiative was taken by the other two powers, enabling Bismarck, as in 1868, to secure an advantageous arrangement without giving the other two anything tangible in return.

The key to the situation is that all the European powers, including France, were apprehensive in varying degrees about German potentialities and anxious to insure themselves against possible differences with her. Austria indicated her desire for improved relations in June 1871; the Austrian and German emperors met (for the first time since 1866) at Ischl on 11 August; Count Julius Andrássy, a Hungarian politician known to favour friendly relations with Germany (D,10), replaced Beust in December. Austria's moves were strictly defensive. There was some apprehension that Germany might attack her in order to seize the German-Austrian provinces; and Andrássy, sharing but concealing Magyar hostility to the Slavs, wanted German friendship for safety's sake and also as a united front against Russia. The latter aim had no attraction for Bismarck.

In Russia Prince Gorchakov, who aspired to the role of arbiter in European affairs, viewed Bismarck's increased status with some distaste, and he and the tsar were prepared in consequence to draw nearer to Austria and even to say a kind word to the French. They virtually invited themselves to the meeting between the German and Austrian monarchs in Berlin in September 1872, which had been planned as a demonstration of Austro-German rapprochement, and Bismarck felt the situation to be too confused and delicate to allow him to commit himself to any decision (2).

Gorchakov and Andrássy however readily agreed in talks at this meeting to maintain the *status quo* in the Balkans, and this was quite to Bismarck's liking. Russia again took the initiative in proposing a simple military agreement whereby Germany and Russia would each support the other with 200,000 men if attacked. This agreement was concluded on 6 May 1873 (6). It had remarkably little practical meaning and was never invoked; in the unlikely event of a French attack on Germany Bismarck would not have needed Russian aid. Russia for her part could hardly have been visualizing an Austrian attack, for the tsar at once proposed a similar agreement to Franz Joseph. The only great power that could conceivably attack Austria was Germany, and the last thing that Andrássy wanted was to give the impression that he was ganging up against Bismarck; moreover, Bismarck had insisted on Austria's inclusion. The military provision was dropped, and in the Austro-Russian convention of 6 June 1873 the two powers agreed (*Article I*) to consult one another even when their interests differed and to oppose all attempts to destroy the peace of Europe, from whatever quarter (7). The German Emperor acceded to this Schönbrunn convention on 22 October 1873. Russo-Austrian interests might diverge over the Balkans: nevertheless, the most important element in the Three Emperors' League was probably the desire of Austria and Russia not to be too dependent on Bismarck's support and to be able to draw together in the event of future German aggression.

(c) *Rome, Paris, and the War-in-Sight crisis.* Bismarck's campaign to secure the submission of the authorities of the Roman Catholic church to the new German state was largely a matter of domestic policy, although it involved the expulsion of the Jesuit Order, the breaking-off of diplomatic relations with the papacy, and increased tension with France. It was not the declaration of Papal Infallibility (formally approved by the Vatican conference on 18 July 1870) but the subsequent refusal of the Pope to restrain the new Catholic Centre party (formed in December 1870) which led to Bismarck's open breach with both. The campaign brought him some unexpected supporters abroad, but in other quarters it was feared that he had gravely misjudged the issues and was allowing them to complicate Germany's foreign relations unduly. The British ambassador, Lord Odo Russell, remarked that Bismarck could not tolerate two Infallibles in Europe (4). Gorchakov told the French diplomat, M. de Chaudordy, in August 1873 that the Pope had made mistakes but so had Bismarck, and that Europe would not allow Bismarck to make the clerical question an excuse for attacking France.

This is the least creditable part of Bismarck's diplomatic career, for both his tactical sense and his estimate of the resources of his opponents seemed strangely at fault. He talked in an increasingly agitated way about the French government's preparations for war. He also talked about a great international Catholic conspiracy, which seems to have existed only in his imagination. On the other hand he was rather too ready (as the events of 1875 were to show) to believe that France would remain effectively isolated as long as the Republicans remained in power. In reply to a suggestion by Andrássy on 17 February 1874 that a continuance of Thiers' regime would have been a greater threat to peace than that of MacMahon because Thiers would inevitably have been replaced by the revenge-seeking Gambetta, Bismarck preferred Thiers, and preferred either to the monarchists (9,i). In a more secret message to Reusz he reaffirmed his conviction that France would fight as soon as she was 'strong enough to break the peace' (9,ii).

The War-in-Sight crisis of April-May 1875 arose from these confused apprehensions on both sides of the frontier. The general context of his post-1871 foreign policy and the absence of all evidence of preparations for an immediate war suggest that Bismarck wanted to warn but not to fight. The warnings were directed against French militarists and against Catholic opponents at home and in Belgium, France, and elsewhere. Exasperated, physically run-down, and increasingly intolerant of opposition, he was giving credence to the most improbable reports. The result was that he was accused of preparations for another war, and was infuriated by international warnings to desist.

Fear of French attack followed the new familiar pattern. Plans for reorganizing the French army were pinpointed in February 1875 by a report that France was proposing to buy 10,000 army mounts in Germany: Bismarck prohibited the deal (10). An article of 8 April in the Berlin newspaper, *Die Post*, asking 'Is War in Sight?' was supplied by a Prussian official, Konstantin Rösslev, and was accompanied by others from the German foreign office, in accordance with its usual press practice. Bismarck later denied knowledge of foreign office inspiration. The article was variously regarded as a warning to France to keep the peace, and as a Bismarckian move to prepare German opinion for an attack on her. Decazes, the French foreign minister, professed to be perturbed. His agitation was increased by a report of 21 April from Gontaut-Biron, French ambassador in Berlin, of some frank comments on the case for a preventive war, made by the German diplomat, J. M. von Radowitz, after an embassy dinner (11,ii). Holstein, who knew that Bismarck had commissioned the *Post* article 'as a means of spreading alarm', was nevertheless convinced that he 'would hardly have selected as a confident a man like Radowitz whose tongue ran away with him after his second glass of wine' (*The Holstein Memoirs*, p. 94). But Bismarck spoke in much the same way on 26 April to the Austrian ambassador (11,ii), who nevertheless assured Gontaut-Biron afterwards that he had found Bismarck in a pacific mood, although worried about the future.

Decazes hit back on 29 April with a circular despatch to the French ambassadors to Britain, Russia, Austria, Italy, Belgium, Holland, and the Pope, calling attention to the alarming features of German policy (11,iii). As a result, Britain and Italy sent cautious messages to Berlin in favour of peaceful procedures; Gorchakov, visiting Berlin with the tsar on 8 May, asked rather explicitly for assurances which Bismarck, furious with anger it would seem, gave him. Bismarck later claimed that Gorchakov sent out a circular telegram with the vainglorious words, 'Now peace is assured.' In reality the telegram (of 13 May) was innocuous (11,iv).

This strange, evanescent affair, proof only of the nightmarish repercussions of Bismarck's reputation, was significant in several ways. France was re-arming; Bismarck's threats and warnings did not deter her; diplomatically, France, in spite of her Republican regime, was no longer isolated; politically, Bismarck had shown that he could be outmanoeuvred, by both his French and Catholic opponents. He was rather ill, raging (behind the scenes), and frustrated. Some re-thinking of German policy was clearly needed.

1 Treaty of Frankfurt, 10 May 1871

Article I. The distance between the Town of Belfort and the Line of Frontier, such as it had been proposed during the negotiations at Versailles, and such as it is marked on the Map annexed to the Ratifications of the Preliminaries of the 26th February, is considered as describing the Radius which, by virtue of the Clause relating thereto in Article I of the Preliminaries, is to remain to France with the Town and Fortifications of Belfort.

The German Government is disposed to extend that Radius so as to include the Cantons of Belfort, Delle, and Giromagny, as well as the western part of the Canton of Fontaine, to the West of a line to be traced from the spot where the Canal from the Rhone to the Rhine leaves the Canton of Delle to the South of Montreux-Chateau, to the Northern Limits of the Canton between Bourg and Félon where that Line would join the Eastern Limit of the Canton of Giromagny.

The German Government will, nevertheless, not cede the above Territories unless the French Republic agrees, on its part, to a rectification of Frontier along the Western Limits of the Cantons of Cattenom and Thionville which will give to Germany the Territory to the East of a Line starting from the Frontier of Luxemburg between Hussigny and Redingen, leaving to France the Villages of Thil and Villerupt, extending between Erronville and Aumetz between Beuvillers and Boulange, between Trieux and Lomeringen, and joining the ancient Line of Frontier between Avril and Moyeuvre. . . .

Article II. [Rights of French subjects in the ceded territories who wish to retain their French nationality.]

Article III. [The French government to hand over all official documents relating to the ceded territories.]

Article IV. [Reimbursements to be made by the French government in connexion with the ceded territories.]

Article V. [Navigation of the Moselle and canals.]

Article VI. [Separate Protestant and Jewish dioceses to be set up in the ceded territories.]

Article VII. The payment of 500,000,000 ($\frac{1}{2}$ milliard) [francs] shall be made within 30 days after the re-establishment of the Authority of the French Government in the City of Paris. 1,000,000,000 (1 milliard) shall be paid in the course of the year, and 500,000,000 ($\frac{1}{2}$ milliard) on the 1st May, 1872. The last 3,000,000,000 (3 milliards) shall remain payable on the 2nd March, 1874, as stipulated in the Preliminary Treaty. From the 2nd March of the present year the Interest on those 3,000,000,000 francs (3 milliards) shall be paid each year on the 3rd March, at the rate of 5 per cent. per annum.

All sums paid in advance on the last 3,000,000,000 shall cease to bear Interest from the day on which the payment is made.

The payment can only be made in the principal German Commercial Towns, and shall be made in metal, Gold or Silver, in Prussian Bank Notes, in Netherlands Bank Notes, in Notes of the National Bank of Belgium, in first class Negotiable Bills to Order or Letters of Exchange, payable at sight.

[France accepts conversion rate of a Prussian Thaler at 3 francs 75 centimes.]

After the payment of the first 500,000,000 ($\frac{1}{2}$ milliard) and the Ratification of the Definitive Treaty of Peace, the Departments of the Somme, Seine Inférieure, and Eure shall be evacuated in so far as they shall be found to be still occupied by German Troops. The Evacuation of the Departments of the Oise, Seine-et-Oise, Seine-et-Marne, and Seine, as well as the Forts of Paris, shall take place as soon as the German Government shall consider the re-establishment of Order, both in France and Germany, sufficient to ensure the execution of the Engagements contracted by France.

Under all circumstances, the Evacuation shall take place after the payment of the third 500,000,000 ($\frac{1}{2}$ milliard). . . .

[Eleven other articles.]

JULES FAVRE	BISMARCK
POUYER-QUERTIER	ARNIM
DE GOULARD	

Hertslet, iii, 1954-62

2   Beginnings of the Three Emperors' League

. . . When the famous meeting [September 1872] of the Three Emperors was safely over, Prince Gorchakov and Prince Bismarck vied with each other in assuring the world that that great event was of no significance. 'There is nothing in writing' said the Russian, 'no agreements were made at this meeting', said the German Chancellor. The real aim, *i.e.* to so emphasize our relationship with Vienna that both France and Russia would have to accommodate themselves to it, had miscarried. The speedy and skilful interference of the Emperor Alexander had been responsible for this; had the inspiration to do this come out of his own head, or had it been urged upon him, and by whom? . . .

Schweinitz, i, 299

3   Arnim wants a new French Revolution

(i) *Arnim to Bismarck, 3 October 1872*

... M. Thiers not only shares infallibility with the Pope, but also loquacity. The end-product of all conversation with the President can be summed up in these sentences:

The country is wise—everybody wants peace—I lead the country where I wish—passions are reduced to silence—the army is incomparable —Europe admires us, and is waiting impatiently for us to resume our role in Europe.

M. Bülow's reports give information about the state of the army.— It is in about the same state as at the outbreak of war....[2]

[M. Thiers'] adroitness in negotiation, which we have used to secure for us the payment of the milliards, is now being used to forge weapons against us—weapons which M. Gambetta will seemingly make use of, if we do not intervene *beforehand*.... The least desirable course of events would be one which would bring Gambetta's party to the helm, in an atmosphere of ostensible patriotism, *after* we had evacuated France.

... I do not know whether the downfall of France will be the salvation of mankind. But I have no doubt about the fact that the German Reich cannot exist side by side with the present French powers that be, any more than Rome could coexist with Carthage or Old Prussia with Poland.

To keep France down in a political sense is therefore our first task, and if the French want to create the trouble for themselves by internal conflict that we have hitherto been forced to create by warlike means, nothing could be better—

The practical result of this is that we can begin gradually to deprive M. Thiers of the moral support that we have given him up to now, and which he has used not without selfishness and not entirely without gratitude—. Once it is clear in France that we can be won over for other combinations we shall not lack offers.

G. O. Kent, *op. cit.*, and *GP*, i,
no. 90

(ii) *Bismarck (Varzin) to Emperor William I, 14 October 1872*

... The whole account gives me the impression that the ambassador wrote while under the influence of one of those oft-recurring moods

[2] The preceding lines of this extract, omitted from *Die Grosse Politik*, are printed in G. O. Kent, *Arnim and Bismarck* (London, 1968), pp. 187-8.

which arise from personal feelings and aspirations. . . . It is not news
to me that Count Arnim is favourable to Bonapartism, and I share the
view that a napoleonic restoration would be the most useful state of
affairs for us. Whether we should set about achieving this, however,
perhaps by war, but in any case by the sacrifice of great financial
interests, is another question, and one which needs mature consideration and continuous observation. At the moment Count Arnim is less
competent to pronounce judgment about this, as he has only spent a
few days in Paris in the last few months. . . .

GP, i, no. 91

4   The Prussian Infallible?

Odo Russell to Granville, private letter, 18 October 1872

. . . It is very presumptuous on my part to say so, but I fancy that
Bismarck utterly misunderstands and underrates the power of the
Church.—Thinking himself far more infallible than the Pope he cannot
tolerate two Infallibles in Europe and fancies he can select and appoint
the next Pontiff as he would a Prussian General, who will carry out his
orders to the Catholic Clergy in Germany and elsewhere. Hitherto his
anticlerical measures have only produced the very State of things the
Vatican was working for through the Ocumenical Council,—namely,
Unity and discipline in the Clergy under an infallible head,—or the
Prussian Military system applied to the Church. . . .

P. Knaplund, *Letters from the
Berlin Embassy* . . . (Washington,
1944), p. 71

5   Thiers fears a German Attack

(i) *Arnim to Bismarck, despatch no. 21 7 February 1873*

. . . In the course of the conversation [4 Feb.] M. Thiers posed the
question somewhat heatedly to me:

'Now tell me honestly, is it true that your government is trying to
seek a new war with France as soon as we have paid? I am sure that

you will tell me the truth—After having negotiated with me the most serious matters in which you have been able to prove my good faith, you would not want to make an old man play the role of a ridiculous dupe. I repeat that I want peace, peace and more peace: and in spite of appearances, the country wants it too. It curses its judges, but accepts the verdict.—So tell me the truth as a gentleman of honour.'...

GP, i, no. 99

(ii) *Bismarck to Arnim, despatch, 17 February 1873*

... His Majesty has described as incomprehensible the fears expressed by M. Thiers, that we plan after payment of reparations to start a new war against France, and he declares himself to be in complete agreement with Your Excellency's reply to the confidential enquiry from the President. Considering his usual intelligence it is indeed difficult to understand how such a fear, for which neither our interests nor our policy afford the slightest grounds, can arise in his mind. We have no other interest than that the indemnity should be conscientiously paid and that France should abstain from further attacks on us. ...

GP, i, no. 100

6   German-Russian Military Convention, 6 May 1873

His Majesty the Emperor of Germany and His Majesty the Emperor of all the Russias, wishing to give practical form to the thought that governs their close accord, that is to say, of consolidating the present state of peace in Europe and eliminating the chances of war that could disturb it, have authorized their Fieldmarshals Count Moltke and Count Berg to conclude the following military convention:

1. If one of the two empires is attacked by a European power, it will be supported with the least possible delay by an army of 200,000 effective troops.

2. This military convention is concluded in a spirit which is devoid of hostility towards any nation or any government.

3. If one of the two contracting parties wishes to denounce the present military convention, it shall be obliged to do so two years

BE D

(twenty-four months) before it can be considered as annulled, in order to give the other party time to make suitable arrangements.

GP, i, no. 127

7 Three Emperors' Agreement: 6 June, 22 October 1873

His Majesty the Emperor of Austria and King of Hungary and
His Majesty the Emperor of all the Russias
Wishing to give a practical form to the thought governing their close entente,
With the aim of consolidating the peace which exists at the moment in Europe, and having their heart set on eliminating the chances of war which could disturb it,
Convinced that this aim could not be better attained than by a direct personal agreement between the rulers, an agreement independent of any changes which might occur in their administrations, have agreed upon the following points:

1. Their Majesties promise mutually, even though the interests of their country might differ with respect to particular questions, to consult together so that these divergencies do not take precedence over considerations of a higher order which may be preoccupying them.
Their Majesties have decided to oppose any move to separate them with regard to principles which they consider themselves alone capable of assuring, and, if necessary, to impose the maintenance of peace in Europe against all attempts to destroy it, from whatever quarter they come.

2. In the case of an attack coming from a third power threatening to compromise the peace of Europe Their Majesties are mutually bound to come to an agreement first amongst themselves, without seeking or contracting new alliances, in order to agree on the line of conduct that they will follow in common.

3. If, in following this agreement, military action became necessary, it would be regulated by a special convention to be concluded between their Majesties.

4. If one of the high contracting parties, wishing to regain independence of action, desired to denounce the present agreement, it would be required to give two years notice so as to give the other party time to make suitable alternative arrangements.

Schönbrunn, 25 May/6 June 1873   François Joseph Alexandre

His Majesty the Emperor of Germany, having taken note of the above agreement, drawn up and signed at Schönbrunn by their Majesties the Emperor of Austria and King of Hungary and the Emperor of all the Russias, and finding the content conformable to the thought governing the agreement signed at St. Petersburg between their Majesties the Emperor William and the Emperor Alexander, accedes to all the stipulations therein.

Their Majesties the Emperor and King William and the Emperor and King Francis Joseph, approving and signing this act of accession, will bring it to the notice of His Majesty the Emperor Alexander.

Schönbrunn, 22 October 1873   Guillaume   François Joseph
GP, i, no. 129

8   Arnim approves of MacMahon

Arnim to Emperor William I, 8 June 1873

. . . All the calculations which have been made as to the prospects of one or other [French] dynasty, have been upset by the possibility that the MacMahon *fait accompli* will be succeeded by another military one.

Therefore if, as I believe, France's neighbours have an interest in seeing that this country is not forced by radical and clerical crusaders into becoming once more a disturber of the peace, and if in this connexion there really is a solidarity of conservative interests, then there is so far no reason to assume that the monarchical question in Europe will have substantial support if a member of the old dynasty succeeds to the throne. And there is therefore no reason to be concerned about this or that dynastic solution, or even to accord it any especial sympathy. . . .

Pro Nihilo! Vorgeschichte des Arnim'schen Processes (Zürich, 1876), p. 73

9   Bismarck determined that France shall remain Isolated

(i) *Bismarck to Reusz, despatch no. 94, 28 February 1874*

. . . I am convinced that the danger which threatens us from France starts from the moment when France appears to the courts of Europe to be capable of making an alliance again, which it was not under Thiers, and is not yet under MacMahon. . . . MacMahon is perhaps not a politician in the sense that Count Andrássy uses the word; but he is ultramontane, almost as strongly as his wife, and can control this leaning and his hatred of us so little that he has not been able to bring himself, since peace was concluded, to exchange even the most common courtesies with Fieldmarshal Manteuffel. . . .

GP, i, no. 151

(ii) *Bismarck to Reusz, despatch no. 95, 28 February 1874*

Secret. . . . Your Excellency will yourself judge whether it is in our interest to see the strengthening of France accelerated. In any case the French army at our frontier is always more dangerous than eventual Gambettist experiments in Paris. That *other* governments view the development of events in France with other eyes is not to be wondered at; they are not neighbours of France, whilst Germany is acting as it were as a buffer for Europe against the invasions of a warlike people. No one can be under any illusion about the fact that when France is strong enough to break the peace, peace will be at an end. . . .

GP, i, no. 152

10   France buys 10,000 Saddle Horses

Bismarck to Hohenlohe, private letter, 26 February 1875

On the departure of the courier I learn that German horse-dealers have been commissioned to buy up forthwith for France 10,000 saddle horses with no restriction on price, with 50 fr. provisions for each. Even if the measure is only the natural result of the agreed reorganization, nevertheless we have no reason to aid and abet a reorganization which bears the stamp of a preparation for war, by supplying German horses. It therefore seems imperative to take counter-measures . . .

GP, i, no. 155

11   The 'War-in-sight' Crisis

(i) *Gontaut-Biron to Decazes, despatch, 21 April 1875*

This evening I dined with the English Ambassador, and after dinner I took the opportunity to have a chat with M. de Radowitz. [Gontaut-

Biron spoke of the concern aroused recently by rumours of war. Radowitz] blamed untimely or over-zealous attacks by the press, but he was sure that it would be a mistake to think of any real and effective action by the government against most of the newspapers; 'the *Nationalzeitung* amongst others, he said, is too important a paper to be influenced in the way you imagine, and it is not the only one in this position. If we tried to put pressure on it and it disagreed, the matter could be the subject of a question in the Chamber and even of lively debates. And is this pressure by the government as easy as you think?— (and it is to this that I wish especially to draw Your Excellency's attention)—what will they keep repeating to us in the name of the parties which constitute the majority? You are reassured as to the present: perhaps! but can you answer for the future? Can you give your assurance that France, regaining its former prosperity, and having reorganized its military forces, will not then find alliances which it lacks at the moment, and that then these resentments that she cannot fail to foster, and that she naturally feels at the loss of these two provinces, will not drive her inexorably to declare war on Germany? . . .[3] and if we have allowed France to revive, to expand, have we not everything to fear? . . .[3] But if France's inmost thoughts are bent on revenge—and it cannot be otherwise—why wait to attack her until she has gathered her forces and contracted alliances? Agree, in fact, that politically, philosophically, and *even from a Christian point of view*, these deductions are well-founded and such fears are bound to guide Germany.'

The Austrian Ambassador very recently indicated to me this way of looking to our interests, but never has the Chancellor's attitude been revealed to me so clearly, so neatly, or with such authority. . . .

DDF, i, no. 395

(ii) *Odo Russell to Derby, despatch, 27 April 1875*

. . . My Austrian colleague, Count Károlyi, called today, and confided to me the substance of a conversation he had yesterday with Prince Bismarck at the F.O. as follows. The Prince, he said, began by telling him that he was not—on his honour—responsible for the articles in the press, especially the *Post*, which spoke with suspicion of the intentions and sympathies of Austria. He looked upon Austria as Germany's best friend and ally, but what the papers said about French armaments was true—the creation of the fourth battalion would give France 270 more battalions than before the late war, and a so-called peace establish-

[3] Punctuation as in original.

ment which could only be intended to enable the French army to take the field at any moment without calling in the reserves.

Prince Bismarck went on to explain in detail the various reasons which convinced him that France intended to attack Germany but he admitted that the military authorities did not expect the French army would be ready for war before the year 1877.

If the French, Prince Bismarck said, continued their preparations on the present scale, and that their intentions of attacking Germany admitted of no further doubt, it would be manifestly the duty of the German Government to take the initiative so as to put a stop to war by energetic measures.

Communications on this subject, Prince Bismarck said, had been made to the Austrian Government by his orders through General Schweinitz—one fact only he had hitherto not mentioned, but would tell it in strict confidence to Count Károlyi; it was that the French Government were having paper money made in England in small notes, evidently for the payment of the army, of which a sum amounting to one milliard, two hundred thousand francs had already been sent to France.

Prince Bismarck then spoke of Italy and Belgium and complained of the clerical sympathies of their governments which only encouraged the ultramontane party to conspire further against the states of Europe, and he wound up by the warmest declarations of his anxious desire for the maintenance of peace all over the world. . . .

F.O. 64/826, no. 183

(iii) *Decazes to Gontaut-Biron, despatch no. 34, 29 April 1875*

. . . The existence beyond the Rhine of a mental attitude not only hostile to France, but fiercely opposed to its national existence, may be considered henceforth and until disproved as authenticated, as it has been put to us by those in whose hands is the direction of German policy. We must not lose sight of such a danger and I thought it my duty to make it known to the representatives of our country at the various courts of Europe. . . .

DDF, i, no. 399, n2

(iv) *Von Berchem (Madrid) to German foreign office, telegram no. 117, 14 May 1875*

The Russian ambassador communicated to me in strict confidence the following text of a telegraphic despatch from Prince Gorchakov of

13th inst.: The Emperor is leaving Berlin completely convinced of the conciliatory attitude prevailing there, which assures the maintenance of peace. . . .

GP, i, no. 182

F

THE NEAR EASTERN CRISIS, 1875-1878

The three-years' crisis in the Near East which followed the rising against the Turkish government in Bosnia and the Hercegovina (June-July 1875) certainly threatened Bismarck's peace of mind; the dominant role in the negotiations earlier attributed to him belongs, however, largely to the realm of myth. He wanted a quiescent continent indefinitely continuing the three-emperors' grouping and French isolation. If Turkey collapsed (he hoped she wouldn't) he wished for a division of spoils in the Balkans which would not weaken Austria or irritate Russia too much. He did not want Austria and Russia to become so friendly as to be able to ignore him, nor did he wish that they should fight or that either should be in such straits as to seek French aid. During the crisis he continually assured the three dominant powers, Britain, Austria, and Russia, of his sympathetic understanding of their problems. But he hardly lifted a finger to help any of them. The documents printed in this section are intended to illustrate these evasive tactics rather than the general history of the crisis.

In Odo Russell's account of a conversation on 2 January 1876 Bismarck professed his anxiety to follow England's lead in agreeing or opposing 'the annexing tendencies of Austria and Russia in the Balkans'. He spoke of his difficulties if the two either quarrelled or became too intimate (**1**). Gorchakov and Andrássy had just agreed amicably to try to end the Bosnian crisis and restore the *status quo* by proposing a mild scheme of reform; Bismarck had agreed, apparently cordially, and the result had been the Andrássy note of 31 December 1875. His approach to the British government suggests that he found acquiescence irksome, and preferred some planned partition of Turkey over which he could preside. France too might become interested, and so think less of revenge. He spoke more openly to Oubril two days later of the advantages of partition, with Austria expanding into Bosnia, Russia into Bessarabia, and Britain into Egypt. Gorchakov emphatically dissented on 14 January. Bismarck then, on 1 February, renewed his hints to Odo Russell in favour of a 'timely understanding'. The British government was willing enough to work with Bismarck (**2**), but as it desired to oppose all change in Turkey, and as Bismarck was too canny to make specific proposals, the matter was left in a vague atmosphere of misunderstanding and goodwill.

If, as seems probable, Bismarck had correctly anticipated the inevitability of more drastic changes in Turkey-in-Europe we can praise his foresight while criticizing his tactics in showing his hand too soon. He did not repeat his initiative. The refusal of the Bosnian insurgents to go home, a Bulgarian insurrection, repressed with Turkish 'atrocities', in April 1876, revolution and the deposition of two sultans in Constantinople, and finally the Serbian and Montenegrin declarations of war (30 June, 1 July), drew Austria and Russia into increasingly tense discussions about Turkey's fate. Benjamin Disraeli, the British prime minister, had his own plans for controlling the course of events in the Balkans. Each of the three hoped for Bismarck's support, and each was disappointed during the last months of 1876.

Although continuing to say that he wanted to follow Britain's lead he warned Münster, German ambassador in London, after Britain's rejection of the Berlin memorandum in May 1876, that Germany could not support any policy which threatened a breach between Austria and Russia (3), and he was not apparently much interested in Münster's assurance in reply that all elements in London desired agreement with Germany. While relations between Austria and Russia were still, as far as he knew, amicable he rejected the suggestion that he should preside over a congress to regulate Near Eastern affairs, on the ground that all parties would blame Germany for disappointments (4). The Russians, taking his assurances at their face value (5), thoroughly disconcerted him by asking through Von Werder, Prussian military attaché in St. Petersburg, whether they could count on his support in the event of war with Austria (6). Bismarck anxiously concocted with Schweinitz, now German ambassador in St. Petersburg, an evasive reply (7), which left Gorchakov thoroughly dissatisfied. In October, however, Bismarck turned down a similar request (for aid against Russia) from Austria through Baron Munch, and he continued to be patiently unforthcoming over the plans of Disraeli (now Lord Beaconsfield) for Anglo-German alliance. His speech to the Reichstag on 5 December 1876 breathed a rather negative spirit of goodwill towards Russia, the Three Emperors' League, and Great Britain, and made quite explicit the German government's disinterest in the Balkans. In a famous, but usually misquoted, phrase he said that German interests there were not worth 'the healthy bones of a single Pomeranian musketeer' (8).

It is true that Bismarck had continued to feel alarm at Gorchakov's attitude since the previous September; his apprehensions are shown in his private letter to Schweinitz of 24 January 1877 (9). Fearing Russian intrigues in Paris or Vienna he clearly preferred to see Gorchakov embroiling himself with the Turks. But he was also going through one of his phases of agitation over alleged French war preparations, and at the end of January 1877 asked the British government through Odo Russell for benevolent neutrality on Britain's part if France, relying on Russian friendship, should attack Germany. In February he asked even more urgently for the conclusion of an Anglo-German offensive and defensive alliance against France. In return Bismarck would be willing to follow Britain's lead in the Eastern Question (10). The British were obviously baffled by all this. Their own aim was to persuade Turkey to accept the relatively mild terms which the Russians were prepared to offer at this stage, and they believed that Bismarck was trying to push Russia into war. Lord Derby (formerly Lord Stanley), the foreign secretary, at once informed the Russians of Bismarck's highly confidential alliance offer.

There is no evidence that the French were preparing an attack; and there is little if any evidence that Bismarck's views, such as they were, influenced the Russian government's decisions. His comments on the draft protocol for a settlement, which the Russian diplomat Ignatyev was commissioned early in March 1877 to discuss with the other European powers, show that he mis-understood the British attitude but was mainly concerned to avoid offending the tsar (11). Russia was forced to go to war after Turkey had rejected the protocol in April 1877; and Bismarck was absent from Berlin on one of his long periods of rest and recuperation from 15 April 1877 until 14 February 1878. He watched the Balkan situation closely, advised Andrássy to leave England as far as possible to take the lead against Russia, and elaborated his day-dream of a controlled expansion of Russia, Austria, Britain, and France at Turkey's expense, which would avoid war but keep them sufficiently in competition with each other to prevent their being able to afford the luxury of quarrelling with Germany (12). But it cannot be said that he dominated the course of events, or that the successful resistance of Britain and Austria to the onerous terms imposed by Russia on the Turks under the treaty of San Stefano of 3 March 1878 was due to anything but their own exertions.

Bismarck's main preoccupations during the first half of 1878 were domestic: he was preparing the ground for a conservative turn in German politics which would involve the gradual abandonment of his anti-papal policy, repression of socialists, and protection, leading to reconciliation with the Centre party, increased reliance on the Conservatives, and the cooling of his friendship with the National Liberals. The French general election of the summer of 1877, resulting in a 'Republican' victory and the final defeat of the monarchist cause, satisfied him that the chance of a French attack on Germany had receded, and indeed that it would be profitable to work for Franco-German reconciliation. He hoped for a dénouement of the Eastern crisis which would maintain the Three Emperors' League but leave his two partners dependent on his goodwill, but this meant a genuine mediation without ostensibly supporting either ally on issues threatening war. This limitation was implicit in his 'honest broker' speech of 19 February 1878 (13).

After the new British foreign secretary, Lord Salisbury, had, on 1 April 1878, defined British objections to the San Stefano treaty the Russian government accepted the need to modify the treaty at a congress of the six great powers and Turkey. Peter Shuvalov, Russian ambassador in London, after a visit to St. Petersburg in May, was authorized to sign the Anglo-Russian agreement of 29 May which defined the essential bases of the forthcoming settlement. Bismarck's role as the honest broker meant that he was kept fully informed (by Shuvalov) of the negotiations; that he favoured all arguments and compro-mises leading to a peaceful solution, but for the same reason had no intention of helping either Russia or Austria with a threat of war against the other; and that he hoped to concentrate Russian animosity on England, in order to facilitate the restoration of the Three Emperors' League (**14**). This was his real aim as chairman of the Congress of Berlin (13 June-13 July 1878). He was only partly successful. Before the Congress Russia had conceded Austrian demands for Bosnia and decided that Britain was her chief opponent; Andrássy had been hesitant and non-committal. But at the Congress Bismarck, in his anxiety to mollify the awkward Russians, threw the German vote wherever possible on their side. The notes of an Austrian delegate, Baron Schwegel, on the Congress show how distrustful the Austrians were of Bismarck's attitude (**15**,i). The Russians, although aware of Bismarck's support, did not consider that it went very far (**15**,ii). The Austrians for their part were delighted by the bold stance of the British ministers, and supported them strongly (**15**,iii). The result was that although the Congress did produce a peaceful settlement, and although the Three Emperors' League remained nominally in existence, Bismarck had failed to bring about a genuine Austro-Russian reconciliation, and had merely strengthened the Russian conviction that he was himself a lukewarm friend.

1 Bismarck suggests Anglo-German Collaboration in Turkey

Odo Russell (Berlin) to Derby, telegram, 2 January 1876

... The danger he [Bismarck] apprehended most in Austria was the downfall of the present administration. Andrássy, as a Hungarian, resisted the annexation policy the Slav party were urging on the Emperor, but if he fell we must be prepared to deal with an annexation policy in Austria and its consequences in Russia. For his part he was willing to join with England in resisting it or not, as H.M.G. might think best for the good of Europe. Alone, without the support of England, he would not resist the annexing tendencies of Austria and Russia in Turkey because he did not think either of those Powers would be strengthened by such increase of territory, or the interests of Germany affected by it. On this question he would, however, reserve his opinion until he knew that of H.M.G. and through H.M.G. he also hoped to know what the French Government might be disposed to do. He would be glad to see France take again a lively interest in oriental matters which might turn her attention from brooding over a war of revenge against Germany. He would also welcome the cooperation of Italy. If he could thus obtain for Germany the good-will of England and her friends he could look to the future with greater confidence.

Germany could not well afford to let Austria and Russia become too intimate behind her back—nor could she let them quarrel with safety to herself. In the event of a quarrel between them, popular opinion and sympathy would probably side with Austria, which would make a rancorous and dangerous enemy of Russia, who would then find a willing ally in France to injure Germany.

If on the other hand Germany took the part of Russia the consequences might be fatal to the very existence of Austria, who would go to pieces like a ship on a sandbank.

There remained neutrality—but neutrality would be impossible for Germany if her allies quarrelled, and would involve a loss of time Germany could not incur as matters stood.

All these considerations he wished to submit confidentially to H.M.G. and to solicit an exchange of views in return, in the hope of being able to cooperate with England for the maintenance of European peace. . . .

F. O. 64/850, no. 8

2   Derby welcomes Bismarck's Approach

Münster to Bismarck, despatch no. 7, 12 January 1876

[Lord Derby has just returned from Knowsley.] Lord Derby received me in the most friendly manner and said he had had a report via Lord Odo Russell about a highly important and very interesting conversation he had had with Your Excellency.

Lord Derby said that since he has been Minister for Foreign Affairs he had not had a report which had given him greater satisfaction. He had a profound admiration for Your Excellency and he considered cooperation between England and Germany to be the only right policy; they were the only two states in which he could detect no really divergent interests.

I got the distinct impression that Lord Derby was utterly sincere in his remarks. [A discussion about the Andrássy note follows; Derby says that England would be more Turkish than the Turks to disagree with it.]

GMF, I.A.B., q. 114

3   Primacy of the *Dreikaiserbündnis*

Bismarck to Münster, despatch, 26 May 1876

. . . Perhaps the calamity of a breach between these two imperial powers impresses the English minister less than it does us; for us, however, as I have already said, consideration of that and European peace must dictate our policy and is in any case more important than the welfare of Turkey. . . .

GMF, *Türkei 114*, vol. xxvi, 1876

4 Bismarck rejects a Congress in August 1876

Bismarck to Bülow, letter, 14 August 1876

. . . The Three Emperors' Alliance has so far been a guarantee of peace; if it is weakened and broken up because of the elective affinities of Austria and England or Russia and France, the incompatibility of Austro-Anglo-Russian interests in the East will lead to war. I leave Italy out of the argument for reasons which would take too long to discuss here. Day after day Germany would be called upon to be the arbitrator between the two hostile groups of the Congress, the most thankless task that can fall to our lot; and as we are not disposed, firmly and from the outset to attach ourselves to one of the two groups, the prospect is that our three friends, Russia, Austria, and England, will leave the Congress with ill feeling towards us, because none of them has had the support from us that he expected. A further danger to peace lies in the direct contact into which Prince Gorchakov and Lord Beaconsfield would be put, two ministers of equally dangerous vanity, that of the Englishman more dangerous as it is controlled by less political experience and judgment. . . .

GP, ii, no. 228

5 Russian hopes of German Support

A. G. Jomini (Warsaw) to N. K. Giers, 23 August/4 September 1876

. . . Marshal Manteuffel brought us an excellent letter for H.M. the Emperor [Alexander] on behalf of his uncle [Emperor William]. It was Bismarck himself who recommended this mission. The recluse of Varzin finally realized the necessity of doing something for us, if he was not to see us eluding Germany's embraces. . . . Whatever happens, Germany will keep in step with us.

At least this will put us on solid ground.

It remains to be seen how this will be done. However, I believe in [his] sincerity. It is clearly in the interest of Germany to have us as an ally.

The French have not been able to understand that, or have not wanted to. So much the worse for them.

Basically it is our gain, for Germany's support is more solid. . . .

Jelavich, p. 21

6   The Werder Telegram: Bismarck's Annoyance

Bismarck, memorandum, 2(?) October 1876

It is almost worse than clumsy of Werder to allow himself to be used as a Russian tool to extract from us an embarrassing and untimely declaration. In his telegram there is mention for the first time of war 'against Austria', whereas up to now the Three Emperors' Alliance could be formally maintained and only neutrality thought of for the most part in the war against Turkey. To ask us for a blunt yes or no to the artful question concerning Austria is a Gorchakov trick. If we answer 'no', he will stir up trouble with the Emperor Alexander; if we answer 'yes', he will use it in Vienna. . . .

GP, ii, no. 240

7   Schweinitz at Varzin, 10–12 October 1876

. . . This was the state of the great diplomatic workshop of the Three Emperors' Alliance, when the telegram and the letters from General Werder in Livadia reached the Emperor Wilhelm in Ems, who had telegrams and letters sent to Berlin and Varzin by the worthy but limited Geheimrat Otto Bülow. One can imagine the effect that these disjointed communications had on Prince Bismarck; first, a telegraphic enquiry as to what we should do if Russia waged war on Austria, then a letter announcing intimate negotiations between these two powers, which aimed at cooperation and division of spoils. Naturally Bismarck suspected that his Russian colleague was making Andrássy suspicious of him. If a disastrous confusion was to be prevented, there had to be an end of this amorphous and dangerous method of doing business, and so I was dragged out from the shade of the centuries-old oaks of the Reinhardtswald. I was not shirking any duties when I went there seeking rest and invigoration, for in St. Petersburg my presence would have been not only unnecessary but an embarrassment.

And so, as I said, I hurried to Berlin, went to the Foreign Office to get my bearings, spent an hour or two with the Crown Prince, and then went to Varzin. I stayed there for a day and a half, spending hours by the fireside, walking or taking long rides through the fields and woods, listening to the Prince, who, however, made no mention of the eastern question; he had been quarrelling with his neighbours and was very worked up, and raged against the hostile Pomeranian Junkers. Then he complained of tiredness, anger, and the hostility he had to combat, and he spoke of retiring. I made a point of convincing him that General Werder, with whom he was in a fury, could only have acted as he did. Then I asked him what we could aim at as a *quid pro quo* from Russia, if we lent her our support; the Prince hinted that we should like a guarantee of Alsace-Lorraine. He made no mention of Poland; I did not mention it either, although I had cherished the hope for a long time that the solving of the eastern question might give us a better eastern boundary. The instructions that the Prince gave me verbally can be summarized thus: we should agree to everything over which Russia and Austria agreed, and in the case of a major war we should see to it that neither country suffered a loss of power. Finally the Chancellor authorized me to go to the Emperor at Baden, and then to go via St. Petersburg to Livadia: he agreed that I could serve no useful purpose in the Russian capital. . . .

Schweinitz, i, 355-6

8   The 'Pomeranian Musketeer' Speech

Bismarck's speech of 5 December 1876 to the German Reichstag

. . . So in the Eastern question we have set ourselves a task: and if I characterize it the questioner will gather that the customs question has no place in this programme, and that he must separate the two things: policy by itself and the customs question by itself. In Turkey we have the interests, which I have already explained, of general sympathy with our fellow Christians, and if the previous speaker quoted a report that he himself treats as apocryphal, that I am supposed to have said that in the whole of the Orient there is no interest that is worth the revenues of a single Pomeranian manor, that is wrong. In all such legends there is a grain of truth, and always a bit of falsehood too. (Much laughter.) What I said was: I will not advise active participation of Germany in these things as long as I see no interest for Germany in it which—forgive the blunt expression—would be worth the healthy bones of a single Pomeranian musketeer. I have sought to

emphasize that we must be more sparing with the blood of our people
and our soldiers when it is a question of deliberately embarking on a
policy in which no interest of ours is involved. . . .

GW, 11, 472-3, 475-6

9   Suspicions of Russian Policy in January 1877

Bismarck to Schweinitz, private letter, 24 January 1877

. . . I much fear that there are influential people in Russia, who would
sooner fight with the Parisian government against Germany, than for
the eastern Christians in Turkey. I fear especially that the efforts of
Prince Gorchakov are aimed at destroying the sympathy of the
Emperor Alexander for his uncle and for Prussia, at upsetting our
relationship as far as possible with Austria and England, and, perhaps
by diplomatic influence in Vienna, perhaps by threats to Austria and
fomenting distrust of us, at overthrowing the Andrássy government
and clearing the way for one which would aim at a diplomatic anti-
German coalition, which with the addition of France would grow
stronger every day. As Your Excellency will see from our despatch of
19th inst., in the sphere of press intrigue we have quite new but irrefut-
able proof that the press agents in attendance on the Russian embassy
in Vienna are busy spreading the idea that we aim to work up anti-
Russian feeling in Austria. . . .

You may answer that my distrust of Gorchakov's plans and the
support of them by Ignatiev and Prince Orlov goes perhaps too far;
but when one is answerable for the fate of a great empire, one must
watch carefully for symptoms which hint at threats to it, and take
counter action in good time. . . .

GP, ii, no. 273

10   An Alliance offer to Britain rejected

Shuvalov to Gorchakov, letter, 8/20 February 1877

. . . A few days ago Lord Odo Russell reported to his government that
Prince Bismarck continued to express to him the same uneasiness on
the subject of armaments and the concentration of French troops,
which he said would oblige him very shortly to ask Paris for explanations on the matter. He asked him at the same time to sound his
government on the possible conclusion of an offensive and defensive

alliance against France. The British ambassador showed willingness to communicate these overtures to London but said that from the very first he had expressed to the Prince his doubts whether the English cabinet would conclude such a treaty. As usual, Berlin asked for absolute secrecy and a prompt reply. [Lord Derby] did not hesitate to give this, in a negative sense, relying on the national feeling of England, which would oppose a transaction of this kind.

Yesterday there was a new communication from Lord Odo Russell, to the effect that he had delivered Lord Derby's message to the German Chancellor. After hearing the explanations the Prince abruptly changed the subject and told the ambassador that Emperor William and he were going to point out to the Emperor of Russia that he was honour bound to declare war on Turkey, and that in this eventuality he could count on the moral support of Germany. The Prince would, however, make this support depend on two conditions: Russia should detach (*sic*) herself from France, and only undertake a short war.

The Chancellor added that he would speak to the Russian ambassador in Berlin in the same vein and give *ad hoc* instructions to General Schweinitz. This evolution of the Prince's attitude has caused a great sensation here. Your Highness is in a position to verify these facts, of appreciating the secret of Prince Bismarck's manoeuvres, and of knowing what was pretended or real in his intentions. I content myself with letting you know the facts, and guaranteeing their authenticity, but asking you to treat them as secret.

The only deduction I can make from them is that Prince Bismarck is perhaps trying to profit from an armed conflict in the East to end the remorse which has gnawed at him since 1870 for not having sufficiently weakened France. He wanted to sell England the support of Germany in the question of the circular [from Gorchakov of 31 January asking for the powers' reactions to Turkish intransigence] and to exchange it for a promise of alliance directed against France. This attempt having failed, he now threatens to drive us to war and to that end give us the moral support of Germany.

SR, iv, no. 12, pp. 746-7

11 Bismarck approves the draft of the London Protocol

Bismarck to Emperor William I, despatch, 4 March 1877

... The document gives me the impression on first reading that Your Majesty's interests would not be harmed if we declared orally that

Your Majesty would be prepared to embark on the desired programme (subject to detailed revision) if this could be undertaken by all six powers without exception. That this will happen I doubt; and in particular I suspect that England will not agree to this purely moral obligation. In any case, in my humble opinion it is not *our* business, especially as according to Ignatyev's itinerary we are the first who are to make a confidential declaration, to put ourselves in opposition to the Emperor Alexander by contradicting what we agreed to in [the] Constantinople [Conference]. ...

GP, ii, no. 276

12   Bismarck on the desired future Alignment of the Powers

Bismarck (Kissingen), dictated note, 15 June 1877

I wish that, without making it too noticeable, we should encourage the English with any designs they may have on Egypt; I consider it in our interest, and useful for us in the future, to promote an arrangement between England and Russia giving the prospect of good relations between them similar to those at the beginning of the century, and shortly afterwards of both of them with us. Such a goal may not be attained, but one can never tell. If England and Russia could agree on the basis that the former would have Turkey and the latter the Black Sea, both would be in a position to be satisfied for a long time ahead with the status quo, and yet in their most important interests would be involved in a rivalry which would hardly allow them to take part in coalitions against us, quite apart from the domestic obsctacles in England to such a course.

A French newspaper said of me recently that I had a 'coalition nightmare'; this kind of nightmare will long (and perhaps always) be a legitimate one for a German minister. Coalitions can be formed against us, based on the western powers with the addition of Austria, even more dangerous perhaps on a Russo-Austrian-French basis; great intimacy between two of the last-named powers would always offer the third of them a means of exerting very effective pressure on us. In our anxiety about these eventualities, I would regard as desirable results of the eastern crisis (not immediately, but in the course of years): 1. gravitation of Russian and Austrian interests and mutual rivalries towards the east; 2. Russia to be obliged to take up a strong defensive position in the East and on its coasts, and to need our alliance; 3. for England and Russia a satisfactory status quo, which would give them the same interest in keeping what they hold as we have; 4. separation of England, on account of Egypt and the Mediterranean, from France, which remains hostile to us; 5. relations between Russia and Austria which would make it difficult for them to launch against us the anti-German conspiracy to which centralist or clerical elements in Austria might be somewhat inclined.

If I were able to work, I could complete and elaborate in detail the picture I have in mind: not one of gaining territory, but of a political situation as a whole, in which all the powers except France had need of us, and would thus be deterred as far as possible from coalitions against us by their relations with each other.

The occupation of Egypt would not be sufficient in England's view to resolve the difficulties of the Dardanelles: the system of double custody, with the Dardanelles for England and the Bosphorus for Russia, is dangerous for England because in certain circumstances its fortifications at the Dardanelles could be more easily taken by land troops than defended; that point will also have occurred to the Russians, who may perhaps be satisfied for a generation with the closing of the Black Sea. The question remains a matter for negotiation, and the whole result as I visualize it could be worked out just as easily after as before the decisive battles of this war. I would look on it as something so valuable to us as to outweigh any possible prejudicing of our Black Sea interests, leaving aside the possible safeguarding of the latter by the treaties. Even if an Anglo-Russian war could not be averted, our goal would, in my opinion, remain the same, namely the negotiating of a peace which would satisfy both at the expense of Turkey.

GP, ii, no. 294

13 The 'Honest Broker' Speech

Bismarck's Speech of 19 February 1878 to the German Reichstag

... Play the German card, throw it on the table—and everyone will know what measures to take or how to circumvent it. That is not practical if we are to negotiate peace. I do not conceive peace negotiations as a situation in which, faced by divergent views, we play the arbitrator and say: It shall be thus, and it is backed by the might of the German empire (very good!), but I imagine a more modest role, indeed—I do not hesitate to quote you something from everyday life—more that of an honest broker, who really intends to do business. (Laughter.)

GW, xi, 526

14   Bismarck backs Shuvalov's Peace Terms

Bismarck to Stolberg, telegram no. 2, 21 May 1878

Secret. On his way to St. Petersburg I begged Count Shuvalov to maintain there that our interests made Russia's agreement with Austria more important than with England. To what extent the results were in accordance with my wishes, I beg Count Andrássy to gather from the following in the strictest confidence. Count Shuvalov will make the following proposals in London and expects them to be favourably received:

1. The southern boundary of Bulgaria would be modified so as to remove it from the Aegean Sea.

2. The western frontiers of Bulgaria would be rectified on the basis of the principle of nationality so as to exclude from Bulgaria non-Bulgarian populations.

3. Bulgaria would be divided into two provinces, one north of the Balkans. . . .

Modification of article XV of the [San Stefano] treaty to the effect that all the powers would have a voice in the organization of the Greek provinces.

Regarding the occupation of Bosnia by Austria, Russia has no longer any objection and drops the idea that Serbia and Montenegro should divide the territory between them. The Montenegro-Antivari question should be discussed by the Congress. In England we have found little interest in the north-west corner of Turkey, and in Russia a receptiveness through Shuvalov, and full appreciation of the Drei-kaiserbund for the future. . . .

GP, ii, no. 410

15   Bismarck and the Congress of Berlin: some foreign comments

(i) *An Austrian view: extracts from Baron Schwegel's 'Notes'*

. . . Bismarck will certainly have declared to the Russians that he attaches greater importance to the gratification of our wishes than those of England—at the moment he is strikingly, even demonstrably, friendly with Andrássy; but I do not trust him and I am convinced that basically he is only working for the Russians. . . . (22 May 1878)

Bismarck pleads illness and would like to go to Kissingen; but perhaps this is only a manoeuvre to help the Russians, whose gain will be all the greater, the more quickly and superficially everything is settled. . . . (26 June)

Prince Bismarck will press ruthlessly in the Congress for a rapid conclusion, as he wants first to go to Kissingen and then to Gastein, and be back here by 9 September, for the opening of the new Reichstag. . . . (2 July)

The Germans, especially in the Berlin air, are all infected by the Russian spirit and at the same time so arrogant that they have no sympathy with anyone. I long to get away from Berlin, with all the longing that men have for a beautiful country and better human beings. (2 July)

(Sitting at 9 p.m. on 2 July.) We discussed the enlargement of Montenegro and the Albanian question. Success was on our side, but the battle was fierce. England, France and Turkey sided with us, and Russia, Germany and Italy were against, *i.e.* 4 against 3. German friendship seems at times very threadbare, and I see more and more clearly how honest are the western nations, the English and the French. . . . (3 July)

> WSA, Schwegel, 'Notizen über
> den Berliner Congress 1878'

(ii) *Two Russian opinions: Peter Shuvalov to N. K. Giers, letter, 7/19 June 1878*

. . . You may well ask why we have so far not obtained any better results backed by the powerful goodwill of Bismarck. It is because we have been confronted by systematic opposition from England and Austria. Andrássy, very cordial, acting the gentleman in his talks with me, becomes a different person when in the presence of the English, and turns into a servile admirer of every word that falls from the lips of Beaconsfield. The consequence is that Bismarck, whose chief preoccupation is to avoid clashes, and to bring the Congress to an end, finds himself forced to tack between the three of them and does not always exert an energetic goodwill towards us. . . .

> S. Goryainov, *Le Bosphore et
> les Dardanelles* (Paris, 1910), p. 378

A. G. Jomini to N. K. Giers, letter, 9/21 June 1878

... And so they are preparing to undo progressively what we have done, and to put Turkey on her feet again more surely than before! I think that is enough to show what we are up against. Bismarck seems to be roused in face of these pretensions. He promises to support us at the plenary session of the Congress, where opinions will be recorded in the protocol so that Europe will know who desires peace and the well-being of the Christians! (The Chancellor [Gorchakov] shares this view.) ...

Jelavich, p. 73

(iii) *British satisfaction: Beaconsfield to Tenterden, private letter, 2 July 1878*

We get on here pretty well, the Congress meeting *de die in diem*, or at least, five times a week, and the intervals between them the assembling (*sic*), being busily, and efficiently, employed by, what we may call, committees. ...

Gortchakoff is not dying, but very lively and always talking: Schou[valov] has shown considerable abilities in his management of business: Andrássy is an English convert: and P. Bismarck, with one hand full of cherries, and the other of shrimps, eaten alternately, complains he cannot sleep and must go to Kissingen.

Tenterden Papers, F.O. 363/1

G

MAKING THE ALLIANCES, 1879-1884

The system of formal alliances which Bismarck constructed between 1879 and 1882 can be explained as the result of a deterioration of the international situation to Germany's detriment or of a deterioration of Bismarck's nerves; both explanations are plausible, but probably only partly true. Germany, even in Bismarck's eyes, was threatened only by France, and possibly Russia. France's strength, relative to that of Germany, had not increased since 1875, and French foreign policy had been conciliatory and unadventurous since the fall of MacMahon. Russia was querulous and inclined to blame Bismarck for her setbacks in 1878; still, she was in no state to fight the strongest army in the world. Was Bismarck's alliance system really necessary?

(a) *The Austro-German Alliance, 7 October 1879.* Bismarck had found Andrássy an unexacting and cooperative friend since 1871. He and his master, Franz Joseph, had shown no desire to revive the Austro-Prussian competitiveness of the sixties. Nevertheless, Austria, financially shaky and humiliated by recent defeats, needed a political success which she could scarcely find except in the Balkans and could scarcely seize by her own unaided strength. Andrássy had done his best to work amicably with Gorchakov from 1873 to 1877. In the summer of 1878, when he was thoroughly disgusted and alarmed by what he regarded as Russian treachery, he was glad to turn for support to the British, who seemed bold and resolute. On two occasions after the Congress, in September and November 1878, Bismarck encouraged the tsar to seek agreement with Russia; both attempts were rejected by Andrássy, emboldened by Beaconsfield (1).

As long as the Three Emperors' League retained any reality (as Bismarck believed it did up to the end of 1878), Germany could avoid a choice between her two neighbours. But if they quarrelled and she sided with neither, each would tend to seek support elsewhere. France and Russia might link up; the Kaunitz coalition (Austria, France, and Russia) might be revived; Austria might be forced to accept Russia's terms. Germany would then be dangerously isolated. Or so he argued. Austria as an ally was not so strong as Russia, but the central European bloc of Germany and Austria undoubtedly would be.

The new factor in 1879, however, was not Austro-Russian tension, which had continued for at least a year, but Russia's quarrel with Germany herself. Since Bismarck had partly provoked this early in 1879 by certain measures (discrimination against Russian grain, quarantine regulations, pro-Austrian votes in boundary and other committees in the Balkans) the question arises, had he stirred up the crisis for reasons of his own, such as to persuade Emperor William to agree to a breach with Russia which he thoroughly disliked (3)? Or was he genuinely exaggerating the danger, as he had done in France's case in 1875? His denunciations of Rumania shows that his irascibility at this time was not limited to Russia (2).

The tsar's sense of grievance culminated in complaints about Bismarck's conduct to Schweinitz on 6 and 7 August 1879, and a personal letter to Emperor William dated 16 August (4). Bismarck, who had invited Andrássy on 13 August to a meeting, proposed at Gastein on 28 August an Austro-German defensive alliance which Andrássy welcomed, although only against Russia. He was not prepared to risk Austria's good relations with England by signing a treaty directed against France. Emperor William hated the thought of a breach with Russia, talked of abdication, and had to be coerced by a threat of resignation by Bismarck and the whole cabinet.

While the crisis was at its height he took the obvious precaution of sounding Beaconsfield as to England's attitude in case Germany should 'refuse to yield to Russian pressure' with regard to her Eastern policy (5), and Beaconsfield took Münster's remarks on the point on 26 September as the proposal of an alliance between Germany, Austria, and Great Britain. It has been argued[1] that the discrepancies between Beaconsfield's and Münster's accounts of this interview prove that Beaconsfield was reading too much into Münster's enquiry. Certainly this is a classic example of how two accounts of a diplomatic conversation, even when penned by experienced politicians, can differ. But it seems obvious in this case that Bismarck's enquiry would have had no point unless he had been seeking an assurance of British support if the worst came to the worst. Although displaying lively interest, Beaconsfield did reserve British relations with France. He heard nothing more, for at the end of September, after talks with a Russian diplomat, Peter Saburov, Bismarck decided that Russian policy had taken a peaceful turn and that a revival of the friendly three-emperors' relationship was now possible. However, Andrássy refused to consider this (6) and the Dual Alliance was signed on 7 October (7).

By Article I of this treaty each promised aid with its whole war strength if Russia attacked 'one of the two empires'. No other power was named, but Article II made provision against attack on either by 'another Power'. The treaty was for five years; it was secret, but could be communicated by joint agreement to a third power if necessary. The recent peaceful assurances by the tsar were deemed to make such a communication unnecessary in Russia's case at the moment. It is important to note Bismarck's evident belief that the treaty was a stepping-stone towards a revival of the Three Emperors' League. It suggests that immediate tactical advantages rather than the long term significance of the treaty were his main concern at the moment. But as the years went by the satisfaction of nationalist yearning loomed larger (8).

[1] *GP*, iv, no. 712, note.

(b) *The Three Emperors' Alliance, 18 June 1881.* Having consolidated a central-European or *grossdeutsch* bloc by the Dual Alliance (which obviously had important domestic advantages when he was turning towards protection, the Conservatives, and Catholic reconciliation), Bismarck now sought to rout anti-German forces in Russia by reviving the Three Emperors' League. He believed that a more formidable foeman than Gorchakov was Miljutin, the minister of war, in league with certain panslavist generals. On the other hand he was eager to encourage friendly Russian diplomats such as Peter Shuvalov, N. K. Giers, and Peter Saburov, Russian minister in Athens, who had had two amicable talks with Bismarck at Kissingen in July on his own initiative. The tsar authorized Saburov on 20 September to reassure Bismarck as to Russia's friendly intentions, and he did so in Berlin a few days later; the result was Bismarck's message to Andrássy of the 29th, hinting at an agreement including Russia (**6**). The comments on 5 November of Baron A. Jomini, a loyal supporter of Gorchakov, show that the Russian foreign office understood well enough what Bismarck wanted (**9**). Saburov was appointed ambassador to Berlin, and the terms of a triple agreement were sketched in talks with Bismarck, starting on 29 January 1880. The basis was the *status quo* in the Balkans and the closing of the Straits of the Bosphorus and Dardanelles to prevent British intrusion. Bismarck made it clear that he could not sign a treaty with Russia which excluded Austria, and Austria was not prepared at this stage to enter a triple alliance with Russia or to throw over the British. After the Liberal election victory in Great Britain early in April 1880, Bismarck betrayed his fear and dislike of Gladstone, shortly to become prime minister, in some extraordinarily vituperative comments to Schweinitz (**10**), which revealed his fear of an Anglo-Russian *rapprochement*. He had to fall in for a time with Gladstone's plans to liquidate the eastern crisis in a revived concert of Europe (**11**).

It was not until August 1880 that Haymerle, the new Austrian foreign minister, had become sufficiently alarmed by the British plans for coercing Turkey to agree to embark on renewed discussions for a triple alliance. The first serious step was the two-day meeting of Haymerle and Bismarck at Friedrichsruh in September. Extracts from Haymerle's account, which is fuller and more accurate than Bismarck's, show that Bismarck was taken aback by the ambitious character of the Austrian conditions, which included the right to use forcible measures against Serbia, territorial compensation for Rumania in the event of Bulgarian unification, and the right eventually to annex the sanjak of Novi-pazar in addition to Bosnia (**12**). Bismarck gave Saburov a somewhat emasculated version of these demands, after which all three governments agreed to go ahead with the negotiations.

It was almost inevitable, in view of Bismarck's peculiar relationship with the other two powers, that he should appear, as at the Congress of Berlin, to be favouring the Russians, who had not forgotten Bismarck's hostility in 1879 (**13**). Austria's feelings were more expendable, for she was the weaker of the two and had the all-important guarantee of the Dual Alliance. During the negotiations Haymerle had frequently to concede points of detail and of drafting on Bismarck's insistence. Bismarck kept Saburov and Haymerle apart; he talked to Saburov but dealt with Haymerle through Reuss. This gave Saburov an apparent advantage; for he believed, a little artlessly, that he could sway Bismarck's mind against Austria and into trust of Russia. In fact, Bismarck succeeded in persuading Saburov, quite incorrectly, that the Dual Alliance did not involve an automatic defence of Austria by Germany in the event of a Russian attack (**14**). He did, however, insist to Haymerle that Germany's obligation to defend Austria under the Dual Alliance extended only to the defence of her territory (**15**). Haymerle had to be satisfied by Bismarck's specific guarantee (**16**) that the dual treaty would remain intact. The main crisis in the negotiations came at the end of May 1881, when the new tsar, Alexander III, advised by Miljutin, flatly refused to agree to the Austrian right to annex Novipazar. Haymerle appealed to Bismarck to defend this single Austrian proposal with the same energy that he had shown in pressing Russia's demands on Austria. Bismarck could not ignore this appeal, and showed his irritation at Russian conduct by withdrawing temporarily from the negotiations at the end of May (**17**). However, Saburov refused to budge, and Bismarck then insisted on Haymerle's surrender on the point. The treaty was signed in Berlin on 18 June 1881.

By the treaty Bismarck again postponed the need for a choice between his two allies, although the limited term (three years) and the suspicion with which the two viewed each other's plans in the Balkans meant that it was little more than an armistice. Austria agreed to the eventual unification of the two Bulgarias; Russia to Austria's eventual annexation of Bosnia and the Hercegovina. The principle of the closing of the Straits was reaffirmed. The danger of a Franco-Russian alliance was removed. Under Article I Germany could attack France without Russian interference, but Russia could not fight Austria without German interference (**19**). To Bismarck, however, the real gain was seen in the goodwill of the new tsar, which he counted on to defeat the Russian 'warmongers', in other words, Germany's enemies and critics in St. Petersburg (**18**).

(c) *The Triple Alliance, 20 May 1882.* In these hopes Bismarck was soon to be disappointed. The tsar showed no clear determination to get rid of his fire-eating, panslavist generals in favour of more conservative, pro-German elements. Miljutin it is true had retired in April 1881 and had been succeeded by a professional soldier who did not seem very alarming. But General Ignatyev, preeminent among panslav diplomats, became minister of the interior, and General Obrutchev, particularly obnoxious to Bismarck because of alleged intrigues with France in 1879, became Chief of the Russian General Staff. For some months after June 1881 the three emperors did cooperate amicably. They supported Prince Alexander in his assumption of dictatorial powers in Bulgaria. There was a friendly meeting at Danzig in September. But by the end of the year Bismarck was again becoming agitated by panslavist pronouncements and by renewed Russian military preparations on the Polish frontier. Gambetta's short-lived ministry in France (November 1881-January 1882) conjured up visions of republican advance in Europe and encouragement of English radicals and the panslavists. Nevertheless, when in December 1881 the Italian government sounded Bismarck and Kálnoky, Austro-Hungarian foreign minister since 21 November, as to the possibility of an Austro-Italian treaty of guarantee, Bismarck did not respond very hopefully to Kálnoky's rather favourable comments. He did not believe that Italy would ever act effectively against France. In his instructions of 31 December to Reuss he advised against a simple rejection of the Italian proposal, whether it was for a treaty of neutrality or one of guarantee. But he thought it best for Austria and Germany to keep their hands free as long as they remained in agreement with Russia.

Bismarck had in mind the threat of Italian hostility if the central powers found themselves at war with Russia and France. In the new year continued activity by the panslavists led him to favour the Italian alliance, which King Humbert now proposed. Bismarck was incensed by General Skobelev, a dashing young soldier, who made a warlike speech in Moscow on 24 January 1882 and a still more provocative one to Serbian students in Paris on 16 February; he described Germany as the enemy of Russia and the Slavs. In further instructions to Reuss on 28 February Bismarck now favoured a military guarantee to Italy against France by the central powers, and said specifically that his views had changed because of the change in Russia's attitude. Kàlnoky, following the line taken by Andrássy in 1879, would not agree to a treaty directed exclusively against France, and Bismarck, who certainly found Russia more alarming than France at the moment, was quite ready for a general formula of agreement (20).

At first sight the basic terms of the alliance, which was concluded for five years, seem unduly favourable to Italy. The central powers were to assist her with all their strength if she were attacked by France; she was to support either of them, if attacked by *two* great powers (21). But in fact Bismarck would probably not have needed much persuading to come into a Franco-Italian war, and the central powers set little value on Italy's armed help. The treaty gave no support to Italian ambitions in the Balkans or Africa. The central powers took quite seriously the value of the treaty as a bolster to the Italian monarchy. But its value above all was to prevent an Italian stab in Austria's back in the event of trouble with Russia. Meanwhile, the secret Austro-Serbian alliance of 28 June 1881 had given Austria virtual control of Serbian foreign policy. The secret Austro-Rumanian treaty of 30 October 1883, providing for each to assist the other if attacked by Russia (who was however not named), was acceded to by Germany on the same day. These two treaties further strengthened Bismarck's remarkable alliance structure, and in 1884 the Three Emperors' Alliance was safely renewed (without alteration) for a further three years.

1 An Attempt to revive the Three Emperors' League

Giers to Shuvalov, despatch, 20 October/1 November 1878

The great difficulties which are hindering the execution of the treaty of Berlin and retarding indefinitely its practical application threaten Europe with the return of serious complications which it is our duty to anticipate. Our August Master thinks that with this end in view there is no better means than that of establishing agreement between the three Imperial Courts with a view to common action, which will establish all the elements of force and the most powerful guarantees of pacification. This entente would appear to be entirely relevant to the international document which we have signed in common at Berlin and for the stipulations of which we are all bound to secure respect. Prince Bismarck shares this point of view and has made most explicit overtures to us recently on this subject by encouraging us to seek especially a solid agreement with the Austro-Hungarian government. It is because of this agreement, which it would be so important to establish, that His Majesty the Emperor would wish you to profit from your passage through Vienna and the conversations which Your Excellency could have with Count Andrássy in order to emphasize to the Imperial and Royal Cabinet how useful it would be for us to unite in attaining a goal which is in their interests as much as ours. [Then discusses specific problems and the Russian attitude towards the execution of the Berlin treaty.]

All these questions make indispensable an exchange of ideas between the cabinets of Vienna, Berlin, and our own. A community of views and perhaps of action, if it could be established, would appear to us to be more than ever desirable at this time; it would demonstrate once more the good understanding which unites the three emperors and without which each of the three empires as well as Europe would see themselves deprived still longer of the benefits of pacification for which everyone yearns on so many grounds.

If, as we have every ground for hoping, your efforts should be successful, His Majesty the Emperor would find it useful for you to communicate the result to Prince Bismarck and to come to an understanding with him as to the most practical means of achieving the common aim which the three courts wish to pursue. Otherwise Our August Master leaves it to you to decide the best means of carrying out this last move. . . .

Russian   Embassy   (London)
archives, Pièces Reçus, 1878-80

2   Bismarck's Anger with Rumania

Odo Russell to Salisbury, despatch, 2 March 1879

In a conversation I had today with Bismarck, His Highness expressed the aversion he felt for the Roumanians in language too violent to be placed on record in a despatch. He accused them of dishonesty in regard to the stipulations of the Berlin treaty,—of arrogance towards Russia, and of insolence towards Germany, and deplored that they were not within his reach, so as to administer the whipping to them they so richly deserved.

I made some fruitless attempts to get him to speak more calmly about the conditions on which he would be prepared to recognize their independence, but he would not consider the subject at all and declared that he would have nothing to do with the Roumanians until they learnt how to behave themselves honestly and respectfully towards Germany. Other persons besides myself have been struck by the excessive hostility of Prince Bismarck towards them, but I have not yet found anyone able to account for it.

I suspect however that the Roumanian Railway question has something to do with it, about which I shall make enquiry and report to Your Lordship as soon as possible.

F.O. 64/931, no. 139

3   Bismarck loses Confidence in Russia

... Then [5 April 1879] I went to see Bismarck; he received me with cordiality, made no reference to my after-dinner speech [of 22 March, affirming the tsar's proved friendship for the German emperor] which must naturally have displeased him, but neither did he have a word of approval for my memoire: he even worked himself up into a rage because the secretary, namely Prince Arenberg, who had made a fair copy of the memoire, had written his r's so that they looked like w's. After he had exhausted this topic of conversation, he gave me a very interesting account of his own interpretation of our relations with Russia; the constant flirting with France by Gorchakov, the endless preparations for war by Miljutin, the advanced position of Russian cavalry at our frontier, the raving language of the Petersburg and Moscow press, have convinced the Chancellor that he can no longer rely on Russia nor even on its rulers to the same extent as before; hence for the sake of a doubtful friendship with Russia one could not afford to have a breach with the other powers, particularly not with England or Austria. On the contrary, with the latter one should strive for a closer tie, which should be developed into an organic one, not to be dissolved except by agreement of the two governments. . . .

Schweinitz, ii, 60

4 The Tsar's 'box-on-the-ears' Letter

Emperor Alexander II to Emperor William I, 3/15 August 1879

. . . the Turks, sustained by their friends the English and Austrians, who in the meantime firmly hold two Turkish provinces, invaded by them in times of peace, and never to be returned to their legitimate sovereign, do not cease to raise difficulties of detail which are of the greatest importance as much for the Bulgars as for the brave Monte-negrins.—The Rumanians will do the same *vis-à-vis* Bulgaria.—Decision rests with the majority of the European commissioners. Those of France and Italy join ours on practically all questions, while those of Germany appear to have received the word of command to support the Austrian view which is systematically hostile to us and is so in questions which in no way interest Germany but are very important for us.

Forgive, my dear Uncle, the frankness of my language based on the facts, but I think it my duty to call your attention to the sad consequences which these may cause in our good neighbourly relations by embittering our two nations against each other, as the press of the two countries is already doing.—I see in it the work of our common enemies, those who cannot stomach the alliance of the three emperors. . . .

GP, iii, no. 446

5 Bismarck sounds Beaconsfield

(i) *Von Radowitz (Berlin) to Münster, 16 September 1879*

[Gives an account of recent Russo-German tension, culminating in the tsar's letter.] These developments and other evidences which coincided with the arrival of the above-mentioned imperial letter have led to the most serious consideration by the Chancellor and compelled him to ask what would be the consequences for Germany if we, after such experiences, continued to resist the Russian demands and so became involved in conflict with this power.

An essential factor in the decisions which we shall have to make will be the attitude of England in such circumstances. There is no need to stress the point that we are not compelled by any direct German interest from giving in to Russia's wishes concerning the support of her Eastern policy. If we resist Russian pressure in this field it can only be because of our special regard for our friendship with Austria-Hungary and Great Britain. . . .

This is in broad outline the position with which Prince Bismarck wishes you in the strictest confidence to be made acquainted and he requests you to ascertain, if possible through an intimate conversation with Lord Beaconsfield, what direction he would propose to give to the policy of his country in the above-mentioned eventuality. . . .

GP, iv, no. 710

(ii) *Münster to Bismarck, 27 September 1879*

. . . After I had told him in a few words the purpose of my visit, and had been assured of the fullest discretion and secrecy, Lord Beaconsfield began our conversation by telling me that he had thought a great deal about the present situation in Europe; he could not deny that he saw with a certain satisfaction that Russia, blinded and dominated by quite senseless Panslavism, was repelling her old ally and apparently abandoning the Three Emperors' Alliance, which had been of essential value to her. England must have and wished to have allies in order to play a part in European affairs; the policy of non-intervention was impracticable. . . . The most natural allies for England were Germany and Austria. *He would enter joyfully into an alliance with Germany.* The main problem involved was France and the possibility of a Franco-Russian alliance. But he could give me on this very point the most solid assurances. France would never attack Germany as long as she saw that England would treat this attack as a casus belli. . . .

GP, iv, no. 712

6   Bismarck reports a peaceful turn in Russian Policy

Bismarck (Berlin) to Andrássy, 29 September 1879

... In the meantime I have become more familiar with a development that provides proof of the efficacy of our united policy. I have direct news from Livadia to the effect that there, on the basis (I am told) of the general impression created by press publicity in Vienna, they suspect the truth about our consultations. They presume that we have concluded a *territorial guarantee treaty*; the peculiar thing, however, is that this report, far from being received with irritation, is calmly looked on as a fait accompli to be reckoned with, and that in the policy of the Russian Cabinet, and especially of the Emperor Alexander, a complete change to a peaceful and defensive attitude is taking place. The triple entente with the two of us is being given prominence again and they seem ready for the exchange of mutual undertakings for the preservation of the status quo in Turkey in Europe, as far as it is in accordance with the treaty of Berlin, and for the acceptance of the Principle that territorial changes can only take place with the agreement of the three friendly imperial courts. Lively satisfaction was expressed over the fact that by the presumed understanding between Austria and Germany the basis of the three emperors' relationship is restored and safeguarded.

At the moment I can only communicate this to you under the seal of the greatest secrecy, as my source is a very confidential one, although also trustworthy. Likewise I can only entrust to your friendly discretion the impression which, in face of this news from Livadia, the continuous concern of my most gracious master as to possible Russian outbursts over our agreement makes on me.

[Pencil note of 1 October by Count Andrássy for the Emperor Franz Joseph at the top of the letter:]
Received this letter today. With regard to Bismarck, I am completely satisfied. But as to the Russian apprehensions, Prince Bismarck does not seem to have understood them *fundamentally*. They are fraught with perfidy, and I must admit that not only as a minister, but also as a gentleman, I would have scruples in recommending to your Majesty, after the experience we have had, a renewal of [The Three Emperors' Alliance crossed out here] an agreement with Russia with reference to the east. If, as I hope not, there should be no 'pure and simple'

acceptance [by Germany of the treaty], I should take the liberty of explaining my scruples in more detail to your Majesty.

A[ndrássy]

WSA,   Politisches   Archiv,
Geheimakten II, Fasc. rot 454

7 Austro-German Treaty of Alliance, 7 October 1879

Article I. Should, contrary to their hope, and against the loyal desire of the two High Contracting Parties, one of the two Empires be attacked by Russia, the High Contracting Parties are bound to come to the assistance one of the other with the whole war strength of their Empires, and accordingly only to conclude peace together and upon mutual agreement.

Article II. Should one of the High Contracting Parties be attacked by another Power, the other High Contracting Party binds itself hereby, not only not to support the aggressor against its high Ally, but to observe at least a benevolent neutral attitude towards its fellow Contracting Party.

Should, however, the attacking party in such a case be supported by Russia, either by an active cooperation or by military measures which constitute a menace to the Party attacked, then the obligation stipulated in Article I of this Treaty, for reciprocal assistance with the whole fighting force, becomes equally operative, and the conduct of the war by the two High Contracting Parties shall in this case also be in common until the conclusion of a common peace.

Article III. The duration of this Treaty shall be provisionally fixed at five years from the day of ratification. One year before the expiration of this period the two High Contracting Parties shall consult together concerning the question whether the conditions serving as the basis of the Treaty still prevail, and reach an agreement in regard to the further continuance or possible modification of certain details. If in the course of the first month of the last year of the Treaty no invitation has been received from either side to open these negotiations, the Treaty shall be considered as renewed for a further period of three years.

Article IV. This Treaty shall, in conformity with its peaceful character, and to avoid any misinterpretation, be kept secret by the two High

BE E

Contracting Parties, and only communicated to a third Power upon a joint understanding between the two Parties, and according to the terms of a special Agreement.

The two High Contracting Parties venture to hope, after the sentiments expressed by the Emperor Alexander at the meeting at Alexandrovo, that the armaments of Russia will not in reality prove to be menacing to them, and have on that account no reason for making a communication at present; should, however, this hope, contrary to their expectations, prove to be erroneous, the two High Contracting Parties would consider it their loyal obligation to let the Emperor Alexander know, at least confidentially, that they must consider an attack on either of them as directed against both.

Article V.[Ratifications.]

> (L.S.) ANDRÁSSY
> (L.S.) H.VII v. REUSS
> Pribram, *Secret Treaties*, i, 25-31

8 Bismarck on the Organic Character of the Dual Alliance

... I was compelled by the threatening letter of the Czar Alexander [5] to take decisive measures for the defence and preservation of our independence of Russia. An alliance with Russia was popular with nearly all parties, with the Conservatives from an historical tradition, the entire consonance of which, with the point of view of a modern Conservative group, is perhaps doubtful. The fact, however, is that the majority of Prussian Conservatives regard alliance with Austria as congruous with their tendencies, and did so none the less when there existed a sort of temporary rivalry in Liberalism between the two governments. The Conservative halo of the Austrian name outweighed with most of the members of this group the advances, partly out of date, partly recent, made in the region of Liberalism, and the occasional leaning to *rapprochements* with the Western Powers, and especially with France. The considerations of expediency which commended to Catholics an alliance with the preponderant Catholic Great Power came nearer home. In a league, having the form and force of a treaty, between the new German Empire and Austria the National-Liberal party discerned a way of approximating to the quadrature of the political circle of 1848, by evading the difficulties which stood in the way of the complete unification, not only of Austria and Prussia-Germany, but also of the several constituents of the Austro-Hungarian Empire. Thus, outside of the social democratic party, whose approval was not to be had for any policy whatever which the government might adopt, there was in parliamentary quarters no opposition to the alliance with Austria, and much partiality for it.

R & R, ii, 255-7

9 A Russian view of German Policy

Kálnoky (St. Petersburg) to Haymerle, despatch, 5 November 1879

. . . During my visit today Baron Jomini was particularly loquacious . . . According to him (and in this Baron Jomini was basing his statement on the fact that he had taken part in the most confidential negotiations) Prince Bismarck, whose sole thought was directed to the safeguarding of the magnum opus he had created, namely the German Empire, had turned to Petersburg in the years 1874-5 in order to assure the support of Russia in the event of a war with France, which Prince Bismarck considered to be an abiding threat to Germany's future. Prince Gortschakoff did not believe that it was in the interest of either Russia or Europe for France to be weakened still further, and had opposed the overtures of the German Chancellor. 'It was after that that he pushed us into the war with Turkey, which has been such a test of our strength, and when he saw us on our backs and out of the fight, he went and secured the support of Austria-Hungary, always with the same idea of safeguarding his creation—except that this time he thought fit to invent the spectre of a slav invasion to emphasize his feelings on the subject.'

Baron Jomini then spoke of the negotiations in Berlin since Prince Bismarck's return from Vienna. . . . M. Saburoff had collected his discussions with Prince Bismarck in various memoranda and sent them to the Emperor Alexander, was then called to Livadia and thence travelled to Berlin where he seemingly succeeded in appeasing this wicked man and paving the way for a better relationship, which there now seems every prospect of cementing. . . .

WSA Geheimakten II, Fasc. rot
454

10   Bismarck denounces Gladstone's revolutionary aims

Bismarck to Schweinitz, despatch, 7 April 1880

[The British election result was] synonymous with the resumption of the antimonarchical continental policy of Lord Palmerston, with the difference that Palmerston had to find the means of combating the Emperor Nicholas outside the borders of Russia, partly even take them from England itself, whereas a revolutionary policy inspired by Gladstone will find the plotters against the throne of the Emperor Alexander already assembled *in* Russia and the neighbouring slav states under the banner of Panslavism. Accordingly, Germany must seek agreement with France and prevent any weakening of Russian influence in Turkey. We are rather more inclined to make concessions to Russia in the east, and were even more so inclined earlier, up to the moment when Russia began to make it her aim to increase our feeling of isolation by repelling all advances on our part. Today we must, to be sure, also aim at preserving relations with Austria, but that will not substantially alter the 1872 programme *for us*, for now as ever our chief concern must be to preserve peace, and act as the mediating and unifying factor between the monarchical elements in Europe which still stand firm.

> W. Windelband, *Bismarck und die europäischen Grossmächte, 1879-1885* (Essen, 1942), p. 139

11   Advice to Austria on the Treatment of Russia

Haymerle, memorandum, 30 May 1880

Prince Reusz read to me yesterday a despatch from Prince Bismarck, the substance of which, according to my recollection, was as follows: According to the reports of the ambassador we seem to be under the mistaken impression that Germany is trying to force us into close relations with Russia, or that she is thinking of adding Russia as a third to the treaty which we have already concluded between the two of us. This is just as far from Germany's thoughts as the wish that we should collaborate with Russia over a general plan for the future shaping of conditions in the east.

Prince Bismarck knows quite well that our respective interests in the east do not coincide. Neither we nor Germany could give such an arrangement a suitable form, and it would seem to him to be, both in 'word and deed', unthinkable.

What he would like above all and cannot sufficiently emphasize, is to avoid letting Russia have the feeling of complete isolation. Our task would therefore be to give Russia by subtle means the impression that in certain circumstances she could have an understanding with Austria-Hungary.

'The various phases of Russian views and desires' should therefore, in the opinion of the Prince, 'not be rejected at the outset', and an amicable discussion not be ruled out. We can be assured that Germany will not be lacking in all necessary caution.

Finally Prince Bismarck repeated that there could be no thought of including Russia as a third member of the alliance. It would be contrary to the *defensive character of our alliance: for he could not see who would be threatening Russia?* . . .

WSA, Geheimakten II, Fasz. rot 454

12   The Friedrichsruh Meeting, September 1880

Haymerle to Emperor Franz Joseph, despatch, 9 September 1880

My two days' stay in Friedrichsruh was used almost exclusively by Prince Bismarck to advocate a better understanding with Russia and to support the wish of the Emperor Alexander that the triple agreement should be maintained, particularly with reference to the question of Bulgarian unification. . . .

Prince Bismarck finds mistrust very understandable, he himself will not be lacking in caution; and thus, against the wishes of the military, he is insisting that the newly organised bodies of troops should be stationed, not on the western but on the eastern boundary, since Russia does not propose making any changes in the disposition of her troops in Poland. But he did not intend to show any mistrust, as it would not help the situation and would only bring Russia and England closer together. The republican movement in western Europe was making undeniable progress, not only in France, but especially in England, thanks to the foolish policy of Gladstone. And so in the interests of the monarchical principle it was a question, not of loosening the ties between the three empires, but of strengthening them .

To bring about the revival of the Emperors' Alliance would be the only way to reawaken in England the sense of her true interests and to overthrow Gladstone, which he considered to be one of the chief aims of his policy. . . .

I [said that I] assume the promise of agreement to the annexation of Bosnia and the Herzegovina; but I must recall that Russia has already declared her willingness for this, as regards Bosnia and Herzgovina already in the convention additionelle of January 1877, and as regards Novibazar, which is reserved for the future, in the Berlin declaration.

If by the Bulgarian union so much scope is given to Russian influence, we must take all the more care, I continued, to see that the neighbouring states are not withdrawn from our influence. We insist on a free hand against Serbia, in case her continued hostile attitude should force us to proceed against her with more forceful means than economic pressure, in which case, however, we would not be motivated by the thoughts of conquest, but only aim at making a good neighbour out of a bad one.

This eventuality could easily be avoided, if Russia would persuade Serbia to adopt a more friendly attitude.

I further intimated that if the union takes place we might be in a position to recommend some territorial compensation for Rumania, as the strengthening of Bulgaria would doubtless upset the balance of power between the Balkan states and would make Rumania feel very vulnerable. . . .

The Prince found these conditions . . . rather far-reaching. . . .

WSA, Geheimakten III

13   Giers on Russo-German Relations

Schweinitz to Bismarck, despatch, 5 December 1880, with marginal comments by Bismarck

[Conversation that day with Giers.] The Russian Secretary of State is of the opinion that that meeting in Friedrichsruh had salutary results, had a restraining effect in Vienna, and proved that your Excellency had expressed goodwill towards Russia; 'the mistrust', he concluded, 'which had been so obvious last year, seemed to have disappeared'.

I replied that this was not the case; the mistrust persisted and would do so just as long as the increase in the Russian army organization continued uninterrupted.

This gave M. Giers the chance to talk at great length about the policy which had been initiated by him with the full agreement of the Emperor and, he believed, unreservedly supported by the Minister for War. According to him the alliance with Germany was the only possible one; their relations with Austria could only be moderated by us; an alliance with England would not be possible; Russia certainly wanted to use the favourable opportunity, which its present relationship with this country offered, but it was only a transitory situation [*marginal comment*: told me also by Saburov, who also assumes agreement of the successor to the throne]. The permanent one would be the alliance with Germany; this was the Emperor's wish, and his (the Secretary of State's) conviction, shared by Miliutin [*marginal comment*: I don't believe it], who goes even further.

The difference between his views and those of the Minister for War is that the latter had apprehensions [*marginal comment*: I don't believe that either] and would consider Russia done for if Germany and Austria made war on her [*marginal comment*: why?]. Everything that Miliutin did sprang from these apprehensions.

GMF, Russland no. 61, vol. 19, no. 377

14 Saburov's conversations at Friedrichsruh, 9, 10 December 1880

... I expressed the opinion that Haymerle did not perhaps wish to enter into our plans, seeing that he believed Austria to be sufficiently protected by the Treaty of Alliance with Germany. ...

The Prince answered me with a certain animation: 'Austria would be much mistaken, if she thought herself completely protected by us. I can assure you that this is not the case. Our interest orders us not to let Austria be *destroyed*, but she is not guaranteed against an attack. A war between Russia and Austria would place us, it is true, in a most embarrassing position, but our attitude in such circumstances will be dictated by our own interest and not by engagements which do not exist. Our interest demands that neither Russia nor Austria should be *completely* crippled. Their existence as Great Powers is equally necessary to us. That is what will guide our conduct in such an event.'

I inferred from these words that in the event of war, Germany is not unconditionally bound by an offensive and defensive alliance, but that she reserved the right to intervene, whether after the first battles, or in the peace negotiations. . . .

The Saburov Memoirs, pp. 173-4

15 The *casus foederis* of the Dual Alliance

Extract from Bismarck's despatch of 8 February 1881, given to Haymerle on 11 February

The final sentence in no. 2 of the Austrian plan: 'You will consider this casus foederis as unchanged. If Russia, after the breakdown of mediation, should proceed to an attack against the military power of His Majesty' is not applicable, in so far that it has not hitherto been part of the casus foederis to cover military forces stationed outside Austro-Hungarian or German territory. It is not clear how Austria-Hungary within the provisions of our alliance could be in a position where her military power and her territories did not coincide.

The extension of the alliance of 1879 implied in the formula quoted would create difficulties for me similar to those which we had to overcome a year and a half ago, and I should fight for the extension with less conviction, as it would not be supported by the same weight of public opinion here at home, as the present purely defensive alliance with Austria. We should be overstepping the bounds of defensive action, if a preliminary aggressive move by the Austrian military powers should be considered as the basis of the new casus foederis.

Prince Bismarck cannot see either how Austria could derive substantial benefit from a false extension, but a substantial disadvantage from its omission. The report in effect makes the assumption that Russia would have gone into Moldavia, and hence Austria into Wallachia. The Chancellor would find the latter natural in the circumstances, as also the occupation of Serbia; but he cannot see why Austria would need Germany to defend a position taken up there. An attack by Russia merely on Austrian forces in Wallachia is not likely in such a case, and from a military point of view has little prospect of success. Austria alone could fend it off, if Austria were not simultaneously attacked elsewhere, *e.g.* at Cracow; and then the casus foederis would arise of itself. And in the scarcely credible eventuality that

Austrian military power, especially if Turkey were threatened at the same time by Russia, were not strong enough by itself to hold Wallachia against Russia, the Hungarian frontier would have to be defended by us against Russian attack. What it comes to is that, even without treaty obligations, we should not leave Austria without support unless she were strong enough by herself. As soon as there were doubts about that, we should have to come in, if not according to the letter of the agreement of 1879, at least from general political necessity, as would have happened in 1877 if the same situation had arisen then. . . .

WSA, GIV (1881)

16   Ministerial Declaration by Bismarck, 18 May 1881

. . . the prospective Triple Agreement can under no circumstances prejudice the [Austro-German] Treaty of Alliance of 7 October 1879; the latter, on the contrary, remains binding, as if the former did not exist, and shall be executed according to its contents and the intentions of the two treaty-making Powers;

that the Treaty of 7 October 1879 therefore continues to determine the relations of the two Powers without undergoing limitation or alteration in any point whatsoever through the prospective new Treaty with Russia. . . .

Pribram, *Secret Treaties*, i, 33

17   Bismarck withdraws from the Alliance Discussions

Herbert v. Bismarck, memorandum, 27 May 1881

Today I visited M. Saburoff, in order to read to him by order of the Chancellor Report No. XX by Prince Reusz of 26th inst, and to explain that the Chancellor can no longer act as messenger between Vienna and St. Petersburg; he must leave it to the two cabinets to have direct discussions about the still unresolved difficulties in the drawing up and wording, and for his part can only repeat the advice which he had already given M. Saburoff, to accept the draft of the Annexe undertaken by Baron Haymerle at the request of Russia. . . . The

Chancellor cannot ignore the truth of Baron Haymerle's remark that Russian diplomacy had repeatedly withdrawn promises they had already made, and that he was exhausted by all this wasted effort. M. Saburoff listened to this in silence. . . .

GMF, Deutschland no. 129, Geheim

18   The Three Emperors' Agreement commended

Bismarck to William I, despatch, 15 June 1881

. . . As the Emperor Alexander is known to be a man who keeps his word, we may look on the peace of our two neighbours as assured for some years to come. Moreover, the danger for Germany of a Franco-Russian coalition is completely removed, and thereby the peaceful attitude of France towards us as good as guaranteed; at the same time as a result of the assurance that the young Emperor has given, the ground will be taken from under the feet of the anti-German war party in Russia, who have been trying to influence his decisions.

I have no doubt that after the lapse of three years, which is to be the initial duration of the treaty, it will be possible to achieve a further extension of this treaty for all three imperial courts, but in any case for Germany and Russia. I can therefore respectfully recommend to your Majesty the acceptance of the agreement made between the two other Imperial courts.

GP, iii, no. 531

19   Three Emperors' Treaty of Alliance, 18 June 1881

Article I. In case one of the High Contracting Parties should find itself at war with a fourth Great Power, the two others shall maintain towards it a benevolent neutrality and shall devote their efforts to the localization of the conflict.

This stipulation shall apply likewise to a war between one of the three Powers and Turkey, but only in the case where a previous agreement shall have been reached between the three Courts as to the results of this war.

In the special case where one of them should obtain a more positive support from one of its two Allies, the obligatory value of the present Article shall remain in all its force for the third.

Article II. Russia, in agreement with Germany, declares her firm resolution to respect the interests arising from the new position assured to Austria-Hungary by the Treaty of Berlin.

The three Courts, desirous of avoiding all discord between them, engage to take account of their respective interests in the Balkan Peninsula. They further promise one another that any new modifications in the territorial status quo of Turkey in Europe can be accomplished only in virtue of a common agreement between them.

In order to facilitate the agreement contemplated by the present Article, an agreement of which it is impossible to foresee all the conditions, the three Courts from the present moment record in the Protocol annexed to this Treaty the points on which an understanding has already been established in principle.

Article III. The three Courts recognize the European and mutually obligatory character of the principle of the closing of the Straits of the Bosphorus and of the Dardanelles, founded on international law, confirmed by treaties, and summed up in the declaration of the second Plenipotentiary of Russia at the session of July 12 of the Congress of Berlin (Protocol 19).

They will take care in common that Turkey shall make no exception to this rule in favour of the interests of any Government whatsoever, by lending to warlike operations of a belligerent Power the portion of its Empire constituted by the Straits.

In case of infringement, or to prevent it if such infringement should be in prospect, the three Courts will inform Turkey that they would regard her, in that event, as putting herself in a state of war towards the injured Party, and as having deprived herself thenceforth of the benefits of the security assured to her territorial status quo by the Treaty of Berlin.

Article IV. The present Treaty shall be in force during a period of three years, dating from the day of the exchange of ratifications.

Article V. The High Contracting Parties mutually promise secrecy as to the contents and the existence of the present Treaty, as well as of the Protocol annexed thereto.

Article VI. The secret Conventions concluded between Germany and Russia and between Austria-Hungary and Russia in 1873 are replaced by the present Treaty.

Article VII. [Ratifications.]

SEPARATE PROTOCOL TO THE THREE EMPERORS' CONVENTION, 18 JUNE 1881

1. Bosnia and Herzegovina.
Austria-Hungary reserves the right to annex these provinces at whatever moment she shall judge opportune.

2. Sandjak of Novibazar.
The Declaration exchanged between the Austro-Hungarian Plenipotentiaries and the Russian Plenipotentiaries at the Congress of Berlin under date of July 13/1 1878 remains in force.

3. Eastern Rumelia.
The three Powers agree in regarding the eventuality of an occupation either of Eastern Rumelia or of the Balkans as full of perils for the general peace. In case this should occur, they will employ their efforts to dissuade the Porte from such an enterprise, it being well understood that Bulgaria and Eastern Rumelia on their part are to abstain from provoking the Porte by attacks emanating from their territories against the other provinces of the Ottoman Empire.

4. Bulgaria.
The three Powers will not oppose the eventual reunion of Bulgaria and Eastern Rumelia within the territorial limits assigned to them by the Treaty of Berlin, if this question should come up by the force of circumstances. They agree to dissuade the Bulgarians from all aggression against the neighbouring provinces, particularly Macedonia, and to inform them that in such a case they would be acting at their own risk and peril.

5. Attitude of Agents in the East.
In order to avoid collisions of interests in the local questions which may arise, the three Courts will furnish their representatives and agents in the Orient with a general instruction, directing them to endeavour to smooth out their divergences by friendly explanations between themselves in each special case; and, in the cases where they do not succeed in doing so, to refer the matters to their Governments.

6.

The present Protocol forms an integral part of the secret Treaty signed on this day at Berlin, and shall have the same force and validity. . . .

(L.S.) BISMARCK
(L.S.) SZÉCHÉNYI
(L.S.) SABOUROFF

GP, iii, no. 532

20   Bismarck authorizes the Conclusion of the Triple Alliance

K. A. Busch (Under-Secretary of State) to Reuz, 16 March 1882

Concerning your esteemed report no. 112 of 10th inst., the Chancellor remarked that it was not his intention to propose any formula for the agreement with Italy, which is directed exclusively against France. He only wanted to emphasize that in fact Italy was threatened first and foremost by France, and that therefore a mere treaty of neutrality or an agreement, which offers no security against a French attack, could not satisfy the needs of Italy. The Chancellor therefore begs Your Excellency to tell Kálnoky, that he for his part would have no objection to a general formula in the agreement, especially as in the present circumstances Russia seems to be ahead of France on the slippery path to war.

With reference to Count Kálnoky's statement that Austria has nothing to fear from France, the Chancellor thinks that this does not accord with history. If Austria is involved in war with Russia and Germany is dragged in, the danger that France would turn against both Germany *and* Austria would not be remote.

GP, iii, no. 553

21   Triple Alliance Treaty between Germany, Austria-Hungary, and Italy, 20 May 1882

. . . *Article I.* The High Contracting Parties mutually promise peace and friendship, and will enter into no alliance or engagement directed against any one of Their States.

They engage to proceed to an exchange of ideas on the political and economic questions of a general nature which may arise, and they further promise one another their mutual support within the limits of their own interests.

Article II. In case Italy, without direct provocation on her part, should be attacked by France for any reason whatsoever, the two other Contracting Parties shall be bound to lend help and assistance with all Their forces to the Party attacked.

This same obligation shall devolve upon Italy in case of any aggression without direct provocation by France against Germany.

Article III. If one, or two, of the High Contracting Parties, without direct provocation on their part, should chance to be attacked and to be engaged in a war with two or more Great Powers nonsignatory to the present Treaty, the *casus foederis* will arise simultaneously for all the High Contracting Parties.

Article IV. In case a Great Power nonsignatory to the present Treaty should threaten the security of the states of one of the High Contracting Parties, and the threatened Party should find itself forced on that account to make war against it, the two others bind themselves to observe towards their Ally a benevolent neutrality. Each of them reserves to itself, in this case, the right to take part in the war, if it should see fit, to make common cause with its Ally.

Article V. If the peace of any of the High Contracting Parties should chance to be threatened under the circumstances foreseen by the preceding Articles, the High Contracting Parties shall take counsel together in ample time as to the military measures to be taken with a view to eventual cooperation.

They engage henceforward, in all cases of common participation in a war, to conclude neither armistice, nor peace, nor treaty, except by common agreement among themselves.

Article VI. The High Contracting Parties mutually promise secrecy as to the contents and existence of the present Treaty.

Article VII. The Present Treaty shall remain in force during the space of five years, dating from the day of the exchange of ratifications.

Article VIII. [Procedure for signature and ratification.]
Additional Declaration by the Royal Italian Government ... the

provisions of the secret Treaty ... cannot, as has been previously agreed, in any case be regarded as being directed against England. . . .

(L.S.) KÁLNOKY

(L.S.) H.VII v. REUSS

(L.S.) C. ROBILANT

Pribram, *Secret Treaties*, i, 65-71

H

BISMARCK'S COLONIAL POLICY

Germany acquired the beginnings of a colonial empire in 1884-5, at the cost of animosity (never subsequently quite removed) between herself and Great Britain. Bismarck claimed, however, in January 1889, that he had 'never been a colonial man', and that whatever he had done in the colonial field had been a reluctant surrender to the pressure of public opinion (J,5). This is not borne out by the evidence, which suggests that in the seventies and early eighties he was already ahead of opinion in his efforts to encourage and profit from overseas development.

He had no intention at any time of supporting overseas activities which would weaken Germany's armed strength in Europe, and he relied until 1879 on the National Liberals, who favoured *laissez faire* economics and anti-colonial policies. Yet from the start he was very alert in defending the dignity of the new Germany and the interests of German traders overseas. An interesting early example is his close cooperation with Great Britain in opposing Spanish designs on the Sulu islands in the southern Phillipines, and his deployment of German warships for the protection of German traders (1873-5) in the Pacific (1, 2). He told a group of merchants who favoured a German colony and protectorate in the Transvaal in 1876 that the time for this was not yet ripe, but that he had hopes that in nine or ten years a deep-seated national movement in favour of colonization might have been created.[1]

The statement reveals the growing interest in governmental direction of economic policy which led to his decision in favour of protection in 1879 and to his estrangement from the National Liberals. A series of commercial treaties between 1876 and 1879 strengthened the rights of German traders in the Tongan group, Samoa, and other islands, mainly in the Pacific. Germany secured a naval station on the Vavao Islands (Tongan group), and coaling stations elsewhere. Friendly relations with Great Britain were a convenience, for her free trade policy made it generally possible for German merchants to trade and enjoy some protection under the British flag. Nevertheless he reacted sharply to the treatment of German settlers in Fiji, who had been evicted from their holdings after the British annexation of the island in 1874, allegedly for infringement of local debt regulations. His protest to London met with a

[1] M. E. Townsend, *The Rise and Fall of Germany's Colonial Empire* (New York, 1930), p. 68.

temporizing reply. When the Hamburg firm of Godeffroy, which had established a monopoly of the trade of Samoa, found itself faced with bankruptcy in 1879, Bismarck proposed a subsidy to prevent a British takeover by Barings.

These developments show his interest at a time when the tide was only beginning to turn against anti-colonialism in Germany and elsewhere. The anti-colonial majority of the Reichstag secured the rejection of the Samoan Subsidy bill in April 1880. He was evidently alive to the economic possibilities of trade and influence in those vast areas of Africa and Asia which had not yet come under European sovereignty, and in which limited territorial footholds (trading posts, coaling stations etc.) were sometimes a convenience. On the other hand he had shown no interest in the acquisition of control over large native populations in order to monopolize markets and supplies, still less for more ambitious empire building (3). He wished, moreover, to increase the margin of German political preponderance in Europe by encouraging Russia and France to dissipate their energies outside Europe, Russia entangling herself in disputes with Great Britain in Asia (and checkmated by Austria in the Balkans), France expanding in north-west Africa to the annoyance of Italy and herself exasperated by Britain's occupation of Egypt in 1882. He did not wish to take sides in these disputes. His mediation was intended to earn goodwill, and keep the issues simmering (cf. F, 12).

Things took a more violent turn in 1884 mainly because he felt himself thwarted by the British government at the time when he had discerned in the colonial movement the possibilities of electoral support. He was unusually free from trouble with Russia and France in 1884. He had been preparing the way for some time. While supporting British policy in Egypt he expected a friendly British attitude to his own modest moves, and it does not appear to have occurred to the British that a bargain was involved.

Of the four main elements in his colonial policy, two—encouragement of German overseas trade and recognition of the popular appeal of colonial gains —existed long before his personal exasperation with Britain became manifest at the beginning of 1884. In turn, this precedes his plans for cooperation with France against her, which only begin to emerge in April 1884 (5). We must regard these pro-French plans as primarily a means of bolstering his anti-British policy and of completing Britain's isolation, although the incidental general advantages of a *rapprochement* with France were obviously present too.

Bismarck's lack of specialized knowledge of colonial affairs complicated matters; it probably explains some of his roundabout proposals and he seems to have been unaware of the full implications of the word 'protection'. In November 1880, when asked to 'protect' German missionaries in south-west Africa, the British had disclaimed responsibility beyond the territory of Walfisch Bay. A German warship was sent to south-west Africa in August 1881 to protect the missionaries. In February 1883, after privately promising to protect the establishments of the German merchant Lüderitz at Angra Pequena, Bismarck asked whether Britain claimed any authority over the region in question, which was over 200 kilometres south of Walfisch Bay. The British government replied that it must look into the claims of the Cape Colony in the region, and then, after a long delay and reminders from Berlin, replied in November 1883 that any claim to sovereignty by a foreign power along the whole coast from Portuguese Angola would infringe Britain's legitimate rights. On 31 December Bismarck asked more sharply how Britain justified such a claim; the matter was referred to the Cape government, and its delayed reply of 29 May 1884 recommended British annexation of the coast as far as Walfisch Bay! There was a reasonable explanation of this apparently dog-in-the-manger attitude. The British government continued to assume that Bismarck had no desire for colonial territory. It had no desire itself to annex the barren expanse of south-west Africa, but did not want a powerful European neighbour so near the Cape Colony. And although Odo Russell warned Granville in May 1883 that Bismarck would soon be strongly urging German claims in Fiji and elsewhere he failed (down to his death in August 1884) to understand that Bismarck now really did want some colonial territory. Münster similarly failed in understanding for some time.

It seems evident that Bismarck, in the early months of 1884, believed Britain to be isolated and embarrassed in world politics, but also to be determined to thwart Germany's plans. In a despatch to Schweinitz of 26 February (4), and in conversation with the French ambassador, M. de Courcel, on 24 April (5), he spoke vituperatively about Gladstone's incompetence: on 24 April he also declared the Lüderitz settlement to be under German imperial protection. He regarded the Anglo-Portuguese treaty of 26 February 1884 as a British attempt to secure control of the Congo, whereas it was basically a defensive move on Britain's part to frustrate French attempts at exclusive control. On 5 May Bismarck sent two despatches to Münster. One instructed him to tell Granville that the Anglo-Portuguese treaty must be replaced by a new one. The other was discursive and argumentative and may be regarded as a final appeal to Granville to meet German colonial claims in order to preserve German friendship. It did not mention Angra Pequena; it did, however, hint at the cession of Heligoland (6). Neither despatch or message was given by Münster to the British, although he suggested Heligoland (but not Angra Pequena) to Granville a few days later as a fitting subject for a British goodwill gesture. When Bismarck told Münster on 25 May to say no more about Heligoland (7), Münster apparently assumed that he was to keep silent about all the other points mentioned on 5 May. So May went by without any African concession from the British, but with Granville quite failing to anticipate how infuriating the Cape government's decision of 29 May was to be to the Germans. Bismarck was correspondingly attracted by the idea of joint action with France (9).

The British government agreed quickly enough in June to Bismarck's wishes over Angra Pequena when they were at last made clear by Herbert Bismarck, in a flying visit to London. They recognized the German protectorate in Angra Pequena on 21 June, and on the 19th a mixed commission was appointed to examine the Fiji claims (11). These concessions ensured the success of Bismarck's defence of his policy before the Reichstag budget commission (8).

However, the quarrel with England continued for another six months, for by this stage Bismarck had committed himself to plans for her further discomfiture and Germany's profit. On 19 May Dr. Nachtigal, who had been sent to West Africa in April with a promise of British assistance on what Bismarck had assured Granville was a merely commercial and scientific mission, was instructed to place the Cameroons area under German protection, but to avoid encroaching on French claims. This was an area in which Britain had interests; the British consul, Hewett, was, however, in time to safeguard these in the Niger delta. A German New Guinea company was formed on 15 May in an area in which Germans had hitherto shown virtually no interest and the Australians had shown a great deal. A few days later he agreed with French plans for an international congress to settle the future of the Congo, on terms which he evidently thought would frustrate British ambitions in the area.

Thus the second half of 1884 was a period of open Franco-German collaboration in colonial matters and Germany did secure some colonial possessions but little net gain. It made no permanent difference to the basic Franco-German estrangement. On 16 July the Cape parliament, again misunderstanding German intentions or Derby's proposals, resolved to annex those parts of the south-west African coast not already in German occupation, and this brought the quarrel to its climax. Bismarck angrily refused to recognize the annexation and declared a German protectorate over the whole coast line from Angola to the Cape Colony. Granville welcomed the decision in a note of 22 September. Bismarck also withdrew his support from Britain in the last stages of the London conference over Egyptian finance (28 June-2 August). Writing on 7 August from Varzin, he instructed the Secretary of State, Hatzfeldt, to open discussions with the French for a closer agreement on colonial affairs (10). By the end of August plans had been made for an international conference to ensure three ends: freedom of commerce in the basin and mouths of the Congo, the application to the Congo and Niger of the principle of free navigation, and the definition of formalities to be observed so that future occupation of the coasts of Africa should be effective.

All this was based on an almost total misunderstanding of the realities of the African situation. There was nothing in the three objectives to which the British need object: yet Bismarck believed that she was a predatory power who would be frustrated by them. France on the other hand, with her high tariff policy and hopes of speedily taking over the Congo from the International Association (recently formed under the shrewd guidance of the King of the Belgians to develop the area), did not like tying her hand in this way. She whittled down the terms and asked for counter-concessions in Alsace-Lorraine and Egypt, which Bismarck could not consider. By 12 November he was complaining of disappointment with her attitude (12). On the following day he admitted to the new British ambassador, Sir E. Malet, that the British and German aims at the conference were identical except with regard to the Niger, and he was prepared to accept the British evidence as to their prior rights there.

The Berlin West African conference (15 November 1884-26 February 1885) satisfied everyone up to a point. The International Association got the Congo, but France retained the right of pre-emption. Bismarck had played a bold if somewhat erratic hand, picking up colonies and some popular support; he had annoyed Gladstone and, for a few months, conciliated the French. Granville's defence of the British attitude towards German colonial plans did not mollify him (**13**). Signs of lingering irritability with the British and with references to the recent crisis in the British press and blue books were revealed in his speech of 2 March 1885 (**14**). But the fall of Ferry on 31 March after a reverse on the 28th in the war with China meant a violent swing in French opinion against colonial adventures and dependence on Germany. Bismarck found it expedient to resume more amicable relations with Great Britain, although the new German colonies had to be maintained and fostered. Their proximity to the British centres of colonial power, as a result of Bismarck's zest for a quarrel with Liberal England, was a source of tension and mistrust which could never be wholly removed by either side in the future. And however much Bismarck might seek to minimize the significance of his essay in imperialism (cf. J.**5**) the fact remained that he had departed from the purely continental conception of German policy and of Germany as a completely 'saturated' state.[2]

1   Anglo-German Cooperation in the Pacific, 1875

Bülow to General Stosch (head of the Admiralty), 28 February 1875

It is the task of the Imperial government to support German traders in maintaining the positions they have won by great sacrifice and in the enjoyment of their hard-won rights, and all the more so as it does not have any colonial policy. And viewed from this standpoint we are not in a position to fall in with the recent efforts of Spain, which, based on sovereignty deliberately asserted over rulerless or independent groups of islands, aim at subjecting or exacting tribute from German nationals by limiting direct trade with them to a few places where there are Spanish customs centres. . . .

While the claims of Spain to the sovereignty of the Sooloo Islands are supported, at least formally, by a treaty concluded with the Sultan of the Sooloo kingdom, the varying interpretations of which have led to the present war, Spain's claim, made a few months ago, to sovereignty over the Pelews or Palao Islands and the Carolines, has no formal or material foundation.

After trade with these groups of islands had been carried on un-hindered for many years, and many German firms had founded

[2] W. Bussmann, *Das Zeitalter Bismarcks*, p. 151.

settlements there, the German consul in Hong Kong, in August of last year, announced that the Spanish consul had lodged a formal protest with him and the British governor of the colony against the clearing of a German merchant ship proceeding to the Pelew Islands, declaring that this group of islands, in the same way as the Carolines, was under Spanish sovereignty, and thus trade with them was on the sole condition that they had first called at one of the ports of the Spanish settlements in Eastern Asia open to foreign trade, had paid duty according to recognized tariffs, and had secured permission from the Spanish Governor-General in Manila.

As I have the honour to remark confidentially, by agreement between us and the government of Great Britain, the German and English ambassadors will shortly make a protest in Madrid against this claim. . . .

GMF 28/23

2   Anglo-German Cooperation in Spain, 1877

Münster to Bülow, despatch no. 29, 21 February 1877

Following your telegram of yesterday's date I immediately informed Lord Derby that in view of his wishes the Imperial Chancellor has waived his objections to Article 3 of the Spanish-English-German Protocol and consents to the conclusion of the agreements by our respective ambassadors with the Spanish government.

Lord Derby, who seems to set great store on bringing this unpleasant affair to an orderly conclusion, was very pleased with this news, and especially asked me to convey his warmest thanks to the Chancellor for this consideration of his wishes.

The English minister assured me once again how much he appreciated and desired the opportunity to cooperate with the Imperial government, and expressed the hope that there would be many opportunities in the future for pleasant and useful cooperation. . . .

GMF 21/55

3   Bismarck rejects a Colonial Policy in February 1880

In the evening [of 22 February 1880] had dinner with Bismarck. I [Hohenlohe] mentioned the fears one must cherish of Gambetta. He attached no importance to him, and thought that there was nothing to be done, even if [what I said was] true. At table we drank much port and Hungarian wine. Afterwards I sat with the Chancellor and spoke of many things. The Chancellor refuses all talk of colonies. He says that we haven't an adequate fleet to protect them, and our bureaucracy is not skilful enough to direct the government of such territories. The Chancellor also alluded to my report on the French plans for Morocco, and thought we could only rejoice if France annexed it. She would then be very occupied, and we could let her expand in Africa as compensation for the loss of Alsace-Lorraine. But when I asked him whether I should speak to Freycinet in this sense, he refused. That would be too much. Busch, with whom I discussed this question today, thought that the English would never agree to the annexation of Morocco because of Gibraltar.

> *Denkwürdigkeiten des Fürsten Chlodwig zu Hohenlohe-Schillingsfürst* (Stuttgart, 1907), ii, 291

4 Bismarck on Gladstone, February 1884

Bismarck (Friedrichsruh) to Schweinitz, 26 February 1884

I have read your report no. 40 with interest. I think that the Merv affair is overshadowed for England by her preoccupation with Egypt. If I understand from your report that the Russian Cabinet and Herr von Giers wish to show consideration for the Gladstone ministry in this affair, I would ask your Excellency to explain the motives that you think are governing this behaviour.

I cannot believe that the idea of keeping or indulging Gladstone as a *friend of Russia* has anything to do with it, and would rather assume that the notorious inability of Gladstone to rule a land like England is regarded as useful to Russian interests, and that because an incompetent English government is useful to Russia, she favours a continuance of this ministry in office. One can indeed agree that to a certain extent an outwardly weak and ineffective English government is more useful for Russian interests in the Near East and Asia, than a strong one. On the other hand it is doubtful whether the combined interests of monarchical Europe, and hence also of the Russian crown, would on

balance benefit if England, as a result of the indefinite continuance of the Gladstone regime, became internally divided and republicanized.
. . .

I watch this sickening of England not without sorrow; the chronic illnesses to which France has been prone for almost a century have reacted very seriously on the rest of Europe. The increasing poverty of France, and the dwindling of her purchasing power as a result, I regard as the least of the harmful effects which France has had on the peace and well-being of the other European countries. If England goes the same way, which I fear will happen if Gladstonianism persists, then all the harm we have suffered through France's internal illness will progressively increase.

I would be grateful to your Excellency for your views on this matter, and your opinion as to whether the [Russian] consideration for Gladstone springs from the conviction that England's ruin and even final downfall is something to be aimed at, or whether they are really expecting anything from the friendship of a man, of whom Lord Palmerston said that he was convinced he would die in a madhouse.

GMF A 1226

5   An Armed Neutrality against England?

De Courcel to Ferry, despatch, 25 April 1884

[Discusses British invitation to a conference on Egyptian finances with Bismarck on 24 April.] I asked the Chancellor whether I could conclude from his words that the British proposal . . . appeared premature to him. He replied in general terms, denouncing, in extremely rough language, the whole line of conduct followed by M. Gladstone.

'It is not surprising, he said, that M. Gladstone has ended in the difficulties in which he now finds himself; he has committed blunder after blunder, he is a man completely lacking in understanding of public affairs and of the interests of his country. . . . The most useful condition to propose in order that Europe could continue to have confidence in England would be the removal of so incapable a manager of its affairs as M. Gladstone. But that is something that one cannot say.'

[De Courcel suggested that the important point to work for in Egypt was to secure equal rights for the nationals of all the powers.] Without denying the justice of this observation Bismarck avoided dwelling on it and passed to another subject.

There are other points, he said to me, which touch much more directly the maritime interests of Germany, and of which I find it easy to say a word to you because it seems to me that they ought to interest you too. We value the development of our commerce in various far away regions where our merchants require that the freedom of their transactions and their loyal cooperation shall be protected against harmful intervention; thus in Oceania, and on the coasts of West Africa, we have all too frequently to complain of proceedings which tend, either to arouse indiscriminately against strangers the rancour and hostility of the natives or to call into question, on various pretexts, the validity of contracts. This is what has happened, for example, in the Fiji Islands, where the English have raised all sorts of difficulties against us. I believe you have sometimes found yourselves in the same position. It is far from my thoughts, believe me, to create bad blood between the British and you, for a serious clash between you would be a general calamity. But it appears to me that all the commercial nations would have an interest in agreeing on common rules to be observed in countries where no civilized nation has yet taken possession. You will recall perhaps that in the last century, during a war between the French and English, several maritime powers, on the initiative of Russia, joined together to defend themselves against the vexatious practices of the English navy. They set up what was then called the armed neutrality. Our neutrality does not need to be armed; but I believe that a kind of entente between neutrals, with the aim which I have just indicated, would have great advantages. . . .

DDF, v, no. 249

6 A tentative Statement of German Colonial Demands

Bismarck to Münster, despatch no. 193, 5 May 1884

I am delighted that our friendly attitude finds approval with Lord Granville. In accordance with His Majesty's wishes we are ready to win further approval, if the English, for their part, show any signs of reciprocity.

They would have an opportunity for this first of all in considering our complaints about the use of force against German citizens in the Pacific, and in greater regard for our commercial interests in Africa.

We are of the opinion that foreign trade in all regions, which are not, beyond all doubt and by general recognition, directly annexed by a European power, should be open equally to all nations, and that further expansion of certain powers, as for example the one envisaged for Portugal by the Anglo-Portuguese treaty, could only take place under the generally accepted condition that the continuation and extension of *existing* trade connections should remain unaffected. Only if this concession were guaranteed by treaty would we recognize new seizures of territory by other powers. The Anglo-Portuguese treaty differs from this proviso in that it places under Portugal's very exclusive colonial rule distant coastal regions hitherto not dominated by her.

A further criterion for England's intentions to foster permanent friendly relations with us, concerns Heligoland. As an English possession this ancient German island is nothing more than a foothold for making attacks on the Elbe estuary and the west coast of Holstein. . . . Our friendship can be very useful to England. It cannot be a matter of indifference to her whether the power of the German Reich stands by her ready and willing to cooperate, or coldly holds back. The effect which our example had on the continental powers with the latest invitation to the conference, the probability of a completely opposite effect, if Germany had sought an understanding with *other* powers over the Egyptian question, are illuminating. . . .

I beg Your Excellency first of all to let me know whether you think you could broach these considerations in a confidential talk with Lord Granville, without causing any ill-feeling. . . . If Your Excellency thinks that it is inadvisable, in view of your confidential position there, to initiate that kind of discussion, we can postpone the matter and leave it to my son, who is going to London for a short visit in a few weeks to take his leave, to use the trust and frankness with which Lord Granville has frequently honoured him to that end. . . .

GP, iv, no. 738

7   Bismarck finds Britain's Attitude presumptuous

Bismarck to Münster, telegram no. 1, 25 May 1884

In view of the presumptuous attitude of the English over Angra Pequena, which exceeds my expectations, I beg Your Excellency to make no further mention of Heligoland in your discussions; Heligo-

land would provide the pretext to reduce the justification of our
African claims to the level of our right to Heligoland.

GP, iv, no. 741

8 The Protectorate over Angra Pequena

Speech to the Budget Commission of the Reichstag, 23 June 1884

[Bismarck said that the Emperor would probably issue a *Schutzbrief*,
similar to a British Royal Charter.] It might perhaps involve the
setting up of coaling stations and an extension of the consular system.
These arrangements might eventually be used for other undertakings
on the coast of Africa and the Pacific.

His earlier confidence that German undertakings would feel sufficiently safe under English protection was shaken, not *vis-à-vis* the
British government, but by the behaviour of English colonial governments. He reminded them for instance that it had been necessary to
remonstrate for years at the want of respect for the rights acquired by
German land owners on the Fiji islands before the British occupation.
And recently the Australian colonial governments had not only made
excessive claims to independent territories in the Pacific, but had also
proclaimed the principle that acquisitions of land in these regions
which were made before an eventual occupation should be declared
null and void.

If it were asked what means the German Reich possessed for pro-
tecting German undertakings in far-off places, the answer first and
foremost would be the desire and interest of other powers to preserve
friendly relations with her. If in foreign countries they recognized the
firm resolve of the German nation to protect every German with the
device *civis romanus sum*, it would not cost much effort to afford this
protection. But of course if other countries were to see us disunited,
then we should accomplish nothing and it would be better to give up
the idea of overseas expansion. . . .

GW, xii, pp. 473–4

9 Bismarck glorifies Franco-German Collaboration

Speech at sitting of the German Reichstag, 26 June 1884

. . . In the historical situation which has developed since 1870, it is a
great thing to have encountered this belief and trust in our policy

on the part of several [French] governments, and I can assure you that this mutual trust will persist now and in the future. Thus our relations with France and the French government—even though there are factions and journals in France that would prefer war today to war tomorrow—are just as friendly and full of trust as they are with the rest of Europe, and there is not the slightest fear that a member of the opposition could make difficulties for us with France and its present government by emphasizing the possibility of a war with France. Between us and the French government there is complete confidence in the honesty and integrity of our mutual relations, and the goodwill with which we regard all French endeavours which are not directed to restoring the unnatural situation which dated from the time of Louis XIV. But there is no reason to fear at the moment that French policy has that aim, and I am grateful to Deputy Richter for giving me the opportunity of fully reassuring not only the Reichstag but the whole German nation on the question of a war with France either now or in the foreseeable future. . . . (Shouts of 'Bravo' on the right.)

GW, xii, pp. 489-90

10 Bismarck's Terms for a Colonial Agreement with France

Bismarck to Hatzfeldt, despatch, 7 August 1884

I wish to have news of the state of the negotiations regarding the regulation of west African trade relations similar to those for Eastern Asia. The present moment, after the breakdown of the London Conference, will be especially opportune for entrusting Prince Hohenlohe with overtures in Paris which, although confidential, will bring the negotiations practically nearer. If France seems willing for this, we could propose the drafting of an agreement together, by the terms of which freedom of trade with the coastal strips hitherto under European jurisdiction would be guaranteed for the participants in the treaty. As soon as we are agreed with France over the basic principles to be formulated on the lines of [those for] East Asia, we could then together invite the other interested powers, such as England, Holland, Spain Portugal, Belgium (or one of the last two, if they have not reached an understanding with one another) to join, and provisionally try to make a settlement with those who are willing for it. If England can be persuaded to join, it would be very desirable, but I do not think it likely; on the contrary I believe that the exclusive English efforts to achieve supreme domination in extra-European waters will force the other trading nations to set up their own organization as a counterpoise to English colonial supremacy.

Prince Hohenlohe must cautiously talk over this idea with Ferry, who as a result of the breakdown of the [Egyptian] Conference and the way it came about may have been put in a frame of mind which now makes him receptive to our plan.

A similar need to resist English encroachments on the sea led in the last century to the so-called 'armed neutrality', by means of which almost all the then European states banded together in an effort to counterbalance the English supremacy of the seas.

GP, iii, no. 680

11 Granville on the Cession of Heligoland

Granville to Lord Northbrook, 16 August 1884

I am afraid we shall find Bismarck a great difficulty in our path. He is making use of us for electioneering purposes: he hates Gladstone, and he will not easily forgive the snub to Münster in the Conference,[3] however unavoidable it was. We have really met all his open colonial grievances: German claims in Fiji, Angra Pequena, and the South Sea Islands, but he has a secret one. Münster sounded, or rather told me he was about sounding, me as to Heligoland. He said that the Chancellor was bent on opening a way into the Baltic, that for this purpose there ought to be a great harbour in Heligoland, that we could not be expected to spend the large capital required, that Germany was ready to do if ceded to her, and to admit England to all the advantages of it. He begged me not to mention it even to my colleagues. I only did so to Gladstone, and we agreed upon a dilatory course.

But neither Münster nor Herbert Bismarck ever gave me any opportunity of mentioning it. I have recently seen an allusion to the canal in the papers. About twelve years ago I consulted the War Office and the Admiralty as to the advantages of Heligoland to us. The War Office saw none. The Admiralty was strongly in favour of its importance. Their reasons seemed to me a little far-fetched. The

[3] A reference to Münster's attempt to introduce the discussion of sanitary questions at the Egyptian financial conference.

cession would be unpopular in itself, and still more so on account of
the obvious submission to the Chancellor. Gladstone, Derby, and I
would not be the best people to make it. But it sometimes occurs to
me whether it would not be a price worth paying, if it could secure a
perfectly satisfactory end to the Egyptian financial mess.

> Lord E. Fitzmaurice, *The Life of
> Lord Granville, 1815-1891*
> (London, 1905), ii, 361-2

12 The French are Unresponsive

De Courcel to Ferry, telegram, 12 November 1884

In the conversation I had with him today, Prince Bismarck showed a
certain lack of confidence in the intentions of France towards Germany.
He took as his text the reserve that we want to maintain in the Congo
Conference in order to denounce the presistent preoccupations which
would prevent us from openly siding with Germany in matters of such
small importance as that of Central Africa. Above all he acknowledged,
when I directly challenged him, that our discussions with England on
Chinese affairs had not inspired him with encouraging thoughts in our
direction. . . .

Passing to Egypt, Prince Bismarck told me that the English seemed
disposed to make pecuniary sacrifices, and that that was right. I made
him see that if they envisaged such a prospect, it was with the idea of
reserving for themselves a guaranteed position which would be the
equivalent of a mortgage on Egypt, and that I thought such a scheme
was difficult to reconcile with the rights claimed by other nations; I
added moreover that in this event France would not act independently
of the rest of Europe, and that if Europe, guided by Germany, left the
territory free for the English, she would acquiesce, having decided in
advance to wait and see what the other governments did. Prince
Bismarck replied that Germany would do little: and that indeed, if
she had seen at her side a France ready to forget the past and adopt
frankly a policy of (self)interest, she (Germany) would have supported
her, but that she could not risk bad relations with England in the
present state of mind of France. He then repeated to me that he was
not distrustful, only discouraged, and that it was with regret that he
declared his difficulty in winning over France. . . .

> *DDF*, v, no. 450

13 Granville affirms his Consideration for German Colonization

Granville to Sir E. Malet, despatch, 7 February 1885

... The belief of Prince Bismarck, that the policy of her Majesty's Government has been intentionally hostile to German colonization, is so devoid of any real foundation that I think it desirable to enter at some length into the history of the case from the British point of view.

I may begin by stating that the despatch of Prince Bismarck to Count Münster of the 5th May, containing an exposition of the policy of Germany as to colonization, and of the understanding which he desired to bring about between England and Germany, was never communicated to me.

Until the receipt of a report from Lord Ampthill of the 14th June last of conversations he had had with Prince Bismarck, and up to the interviews which I had about the same time with Count Herbert Bismarck, I was under the belief that the Chancellor was personally opposed to German colonization.

The reports of Lord Ampthill were continuously and strongly to that effect, and on the 15th March 1884, his Excellency, referring to the agitation on the subject among the shipping and commercial claims in Germany, stated that it was well known that the Prince was absolutely opposed to their ardent desire for the acquisition of Colonies by Germany, and was determined to combat and oppose their growing influence.

The anxiety expressed by Count Münster on behalf of his Government, that German subjects should be protected at Angra Pequena, in no way removed the misapprehension on my part.

But after the information received in June, Lord Derby and I, together with our colleagues, desired to meet the Prince's views with regard to Angra Pequena in every way compatible with the private rights of British subjects, and I know not how it can be said that we departed from that course. [Then discusses British policy in relation to Santa Lucia Bay, Pondoland, and the Oil River Protectorates. He proposes to deal with the question of New Guinea separately.]

I have only now to observe upon the remark which has been attributed to me, to the effect that the attitude of Germany on the Colonial question made it difficult for me to be conciliatory on other points. I have never used any threat to obstruct the Colonial policy of Germany or conveyed anything more than the mere fact that the recent attitude of Germany as to Egypt had for the moment changed from the friendly one previously maintained towards this country. All my declarations in public and private, as well as those of Mr. Gladstone and many of my colleagues, have been most favourable to German colonization.

I authorize Your Excellency to leave a copy of this despatch with Prince Bismarck.

BFSP, 1884-1885, lxxv (2), no. 176

14   Bismarck replies to Granville's Criticisms

Speech at sitting of the German Reichstag, 2 March 1885

... Confidential discussions which I have had here with English representatives—discussions of the most confidential nature, which were based on years of acquaintance but which were naturally destined to be reported—have been summarized in official publications and printed. These are all signs of ill-humour, which I do not think justified, and which I can only deprecate. And this ill-humour is unfortunately aimed at me personally, in that in the latest proceedings of the English parliament Lord Granville expressed the opinion that our claims as represented by me went so far that they forced England—I must quote the English words—'to abdicate all liberty of action in colonial matters'—that England therefore in colonial affairs was completely deprived of all freedom of action. The character of this speech goes beyond the bounds of the moderation which we ourselves show in our colonial policy.

And with this is associated our attitude in other political fields, African included, and it is presumed that I myself have an 'unfavourable view' of England's Egyptian policy, and it is assumed that this unfavourable opinion stems from my personal irritation that England has not followed the advice that I had given her earlier on the Egyptian question. I regret that my English colleague forces me into the position of having to contradict him. I have never criticized to him England's policy on Egypt. I do not lightly take it upon myself to criticize the foreign policies of others, and least of all have I complained that my own advice has not been followed. And the advice which is here quoted as having come from me, I have in fact never given. Lord Granville is mistaken in assuming that my advice with reference to Egypt was 'to take it', i.e. to take Egypt. That is a mis-statement (Hear! Hear!) which I must correct, and which forces me in my turn to go further in the disclosure of confidential discussions than I am wont to do. . . .

GW, xiii, 4-5

I

THE SYSTEM TESTED, 1885-1888

All the expedients by which Bismarck had sought since 1871 to establish and perpetuate Germany's preponderance in Europe were put to the test in a prolonged series of interlocking crises from the autumn of 1885 until the beginning of 1888.

None of the other five powers wanted war. Each nevertheless felt itself threatened or affronted and tended to square up to presumed opponents and to strengthen its defences, military and diplomatic. From this situation war might emerge; more probably the peace would be saved at the cost of future tensions. Bismarck, who showed every confidence in his own powers to control Europe at the beginning of the period (2,i), had to resort to increasingly desperate moves in 1887 to maintain his authority.

(a) *Bulgarian crises, 1885-6.* A peaceful revolution at Philippopolis on 18 September 1885 brought about the unification of Bulgaria and Eastern Rumelia, 'the two Bulgarias' for whose unification Russia had stipulated in the Three Emperors' Treaty of 1881. Since then the tsar had quarrelled with Prince Alexander, the Bulgarian ruler, and he did not wish the credit for unification to go to the prince and his anti-Russian advisers. He called on his two allies to join him in condemning and if possible reversing the union, and they were willing enough to do so; but as the Bulgarians refused to be overawed, and Russia had no desire to use force, the tsar could merely glower frustratedly at the prince. The Turks were too cautious to intervene, and the British government (Salisbury was now prime minister and foreign secretary) saw no reason to oppose union now that Russia objected to it. Salisbury suggested a personal union under Prince Alexander.

Almost at once Russo-Austrian tension appeared, mainly because Kálnoky felt it impossible to prevent Serbian moves to secure compensation for Bulgaria's gains; thus the Russians were bound to suspect that the crisis would be exploited to their disadvantage by Austria. Bismarck strongly urged Kálnoky on 3 October and on other occasions to consider that he would not be choosing the lesser evil if, in order to maintain King Milan of Serbia, he risked war with Russia (2,ii). The restoration of the *status quo* would be the least embarrassing solution, and Kálnoky agreed to support Russian proposals to this end on 12 October. In general, Bismarck hoped that Kálnoky would follow as unobtrusive a line as possible, leaving Great Britain to bear the weight of the tsar's displeasure. The conference of ambassadors which began meetings at Constantinople on 5 November failed to agree on a plan for restoring the *status quo*, mainly because of the British insistence that priority should be given to considering the grievances of the local populations. Salisbury had no qualms about stating his objections to the use of force (**2**,iii). The Russians were furiously angry.

So for the time being the Three Emperors' Alliance held together, and it survived the crisis which followed King Milan's declaration of war on Bulgaria on 14 November 1885. Kálnoky felt compelled to show the Serbs some sympathy (**2**,iv). But the main Serbian attack was almost immediately crushed by the Bulgars at the battle of Slivnitza (17-19 November). The Bulgarian army entered Serbian territory, and after further victories the Austrian minister in Belgrade, Count Khevenhüller, went to Prince Alexander's headquarters on 28 November and secured an armistice after threatening that otherwise Austrian troops would enter Serbia and Russian troops would occupy Bulgaria. The last statement, quite unauthorized, became public and embarrassed Giers, while the possibility that Austrian forces would themselves move from Serbia into Bulgaria while Russia held back was alarming (**2**,v). However, the crisis was momentarily eased, and the real weight of Russian indignation at their highly annoying position still turned mainly against Britain. The unification had now to be accepted, in some form or other; the Bulgarians were in no mood to be bluffed into its reversal. Bismarck in December 1885 reiterated his advice to Kálnoky to adopt an entirely passive attitude and leave Britain to face the Russians; he did his best to alarm Kálnoky with the warning that if he stood up to Russia, Britain would leave him in the lurch (**2**,vi).

Russia remained baffled but unforgiving, and after Prince Alexander's loss of nerve and abdication on 7 September 1886, sought ineffectually to impose her authority on the Bulgarian state through General Kaulbars, who was sent to Sofia as diplomatic agent and consul general. It was inevitable that apprehension in Austria and Hungary should be increasingly difficult to conceal, with corresponding Russian irritation. A speech by Count Tisza, the Hungarian prime minister, on 30 September 1886, insisted that no power was entitled 'to undertake any single-handed armed intervention or to set up any protectorate in the Balkan Peninsula'. This warning, much resented in St. Petersburg, marks the beginning of a new phase of Austro-Russian estrangement (**3**). The tsar broke off diplomatic relations with Bulgaria on 7 November 1886, and for the next year or more the possibility of a Russian invasion and a consequent general war loomed before Europe.

(b) *Juggler with five balls*. Along with this problem Bismarck faced four others in the winter of 1886-7. His skill in finding a workable solution of each without materially prejudicing his plans for the others certainly illustrates the Kaiser's later comment on his dexterity.

German relations with France had deteriorated badly since the fall of Ferry. The French general election of October 1885 weakened the moderate republicans, strengthened the monarchist and radical groups, and registered a decisive revulsion against colonial adventures. Freycinet was appointed minister-president, and announced that France's forces must be concentrated in future on the continent. General Georges Boulanger, a somewhat flamboyant figure, notable for his radical leanings rather than for outstanding military renown, became minister of war. He seemed to embody plans for a war of revenge; there was growing popular excitement in France throughout 1886. Freycinet supported the Russian point of view in the Bulgarian question, and there was talk of a Russo-French alliance which found some echoes in Russia. When Goblet succeeded Freycinet in December 1886, Boulanger continued in office. Nevertheless, the French and German governments assured each other of their peaceful intentions.

A second problem was that of strengthening the German army with a revised version of the army bill, which had been voted in 1880 to cover the period down to the end of March 1888. A new bill, brought before the Reichstag in September 1886, was to come into force in April 1887 and to be valid for seven years. The last point lends support to the view that Bismarck wished to use the bill to weaken the *Deutschfreisinnige* party, which was expected by many to form a government, perhaps with Alexander of Battenberg as chancellor, when Crown Prince Frederick succeeded to the throne. The party did not oppose the strengthening of the army, but it was not prepared to surrender control for more than three years. Nor was the Centre party. During the debates on the bill the danger of a French attack was loudly proclaimed in the Reichstag and the German press. Boulangism certainly had its alarming features; nevertheless, the German press campaign had been launched as early as August 1885, before Boulanger had even entered office. The French embassy were convinced that Bismarck was engaged in domestic manoeuvres (1). The army bill was voted for only three years, in spite of Bismarck's impressive speech on 11 January 1887 (5). The emperor, on Bismarck's advice, dissolved the Reichstag on 14 January 1887, and the *Kartell*, the group of parties supporting Bismarck, won a convincing victory. After this some of the tension went out of Franco-German relations, and Bismarck was noticeably accommodating in settling the crisis over the kidnapping of Schnaebele, a French official, in April 1887 (8).

A third problem was that of Italy's relation to the Triple Alliance, due for renewal in May 1887. As Franco-German and Russo-Austrian tension increased after the autumn of 1886 the importance of at least preventing Italian encouragement of Russia or France was grasped in Vienna and Berlin. Count Robilant, who became Italian foreign minister in October 1885, and who had been sceptical since 1882 as to the value to Italy of the Triple Alliance, understood the situation well enough and accordingly hoped for renewal in a form more favourable to Italy. He now wanted the Triple Alliance to include a guarantee of Italy's Mediterranean interests against France (particularly in regard to Tripoli), and an understanding with England, which had been difficult to pursue as long as Bismarck's colonial entente with France against England lasted. Bismarck agreed to both these proposals in mid-October 1886[1] and advised Robilant to seek agreement with England rather than with France (4). When Salisbury proved too circumspect to take the initiative, Robilant himself proposed an Anglo-Italian agreement in January 1887. In the meantime, however, Kálnoky refused to renew the Triple Alliance except in its original form, arguing that as Bismarck would not guarantee the *status quo* in the whole of the Balkan peninsula (that is, against Russian intervention in Bulgaria) Austria could not afford to dissipate her energies.

Bismarck solved this problem by proposing that the Triple Alliance should be renewed as it stood, and be supplemented by (a) an Austro-Italian agreement under which Austria undertook to consider Italian claims for compensation should the *status quo* be disturbed in the Balkans and adjacent coasts and islands, and (b) a German-Italian agreement under which Germany would support Italy's Mediterranean interests (7). The three documents were signed in Berlin on 20 February 1887. Bismarck also promoted Robilant's other objective by pressure on Salisbury to conclude an agreement with Italy. On 1 February he warned Malet that without British support of the *status quo* Germany would see no advantage to herself in resisting Russian desires in the Balkans or French in Egypt. He promised to keep France quiet so that Britain could reinforce the powers maintaining the *status quo* in the east (6). This was exactly what Salisbury wanted, and the first of the informal 'Mediterranean agreements' was signed by Italy and Britain on 12 February 1887 in the form of an exchange of notes pledging the two powers to prevent the domination of any other great power in territories adjacent to the Mediterranean sea. Kálnoky acceded to this agreement on 24 March.

Bismarck's fourth problem was the most stubborn of all: he sought not merely to get through the immediate Bulgarian crisis without war but to keep Russia on the relatively cooperative footing with the central powers which had existed under the *Dreikaiserbund*.

(c) *The Reinsurance treaty, 18 June 1887.* As a result of his annoyance with Austro-Hungarian reactions to the Bulgarian crisis, Alexander III was determined not to renew the Three Emperors' Alliance when it expired on 18 June 1887. Bismarck's assurances of respect for Russian interest in Bulgaria and the Straits were sufficient to enable the Russian government to maintain ties with Germany if it wished, and when it came to the point the tsar, who disliked Boulangism, saw no reason why he should be dragged into a great war against Germany as France's ally. On the other hand he had the deepest suspicion of Bismarck's honesty and goodwill. By March 1887 he had agreed without enthusiasm to accept Giers' view as to the desirability of a continued link with Germany. But Bismarck, who had discussed the terms of a possible German-Russian treaty with Peter Shuvalov early in January, found the Russian terms much harder than he had anticipated.

The negotiations began on 11 May between Bismarck and Paul Shuvalov (brother of Peter), the Russian ambassador in Berlin. Bismarck agreed readily

[1] C. J. Lowe, *Salisbury and the Mediterranean 1886-1896* (London, 1965), p. 12 et seq.

to recognize Russia's dominant position in Bulgaria and to support the closing of the Straits. But he had to accept an unsatisfactory arrangement concerning France. Shuvalov had proposed that Article I should simply provide that if one of the two signatories should find itself at war with a third great power, the other signatory would maintain a benevolent neutrality. Bismarck had to point out that the Austro-German alliance made it impossible for Germany to stand aside if Russia attacked Austria, and he was not willing to abandon the Dual Alliance when it expired in 1889. Russia accordingly declined to give Germany a free hand against France. These reservations were embodied in the second sentence of Article I of the reinsurance treaty. Bismarck thus lost without compensation the free hand against France that he had enjoyed under the Three Emperors' Treaty of 1881.

Bismarck also found it expedient not only to support Russia in insisting that Turkey should exclude all belligerent powers from the Straits, but to agree to Russia's seizure of the Straits and of Constantinople if she so wished. Because of some incompatibility between these two provisions, Russia preferred to put the German promise to support her possible aggression in the Straits and Bulgaria in a separate protocol. The treaty was signed on 18 June, under conditions of profound secrecy (9).

(d) *Bulgaria and Bismarck survive the crisis.* It is evident that two partly conflicting judgments can be passed on Bismarck's policy in this prolonged crisis. One is that by masterly improvisations he maintained Germany's position and saved the peace of Europe. The other is that the peace of Europe was in no real danger, and his makeshift arrangements merely demonstrate the progressive breakdown of his system. A third view, a rather pessimistic one which Bismarck himself accepted to some extent, is possible. European diplomacy was deadlocked with a number of basic antagonisms (in particular, Franco-German in Alsace-Lorraine and Austro-Prussian in the Balkans) which could not be solved without war, but over which war could be indefinitely postponed by temporary expedients. It is surely too flattering to Bismarck to say that 'with the signature of the Reinsurance Treaty Bismarck's system of alliances reached its completion'.[2] Yet he undoubtedly showed his expertise in the game of cabinet diplomacy which seemed appropriate to all the governments involved.

France's cautious bourgeois ministers had no desire for war, and this became obvious when Boulanger was dropped from a new cabinet under Rouvier at the end of May 1887. The Russians were exasperated by Bulgarian ingratitude, but apart from prestige were mainly concerned to save their existing interests in the Balkans against western encroachments. The danger of this they exaggerated, and it was inevitable that the election to the Bulgarian throne on 7 July of Prince Ferdinand of Coburg should be regarded in St. Petersburg as an Austrian plot. Bismarck's secret encouragement of the Anglo-Austro-Italian group continued. He gave his support to the convention which Sir Henry Drummond Wolff concluded with the Porte on 22 May, providing for British withdrawal from Egypt in three years, although with the right to return in an

[2] W. L. Langer, *European Alliances and Alignments* (New York, 1931), p. 425.

emergency. Bismarck seems to have been intensely annoyed when the Porte, under great pressure from France and Russia, rather foolishly refused to ratify it. But Bismarck supported Russia when she protested against Prince Ferdinand's action and when she mooted the idea that the Porte should appoint General Ernroth as regent, although he would not do Russia's work by proposing the general himself. Kálnoky, who grumbled at Bismarck's contradictory course, nevertheless told Calice on 18 August that the Austro-German alliance was not in any way threatened by Bismarck's evident anxiety to keep Russia and France apart (**10**).

What is surprising is not this real if limited support by Bismarck of the Russians, but his failure to exert himself further on their behalf. He soon became angry at renewed Russian press attacks, reports of military concentrations on the Polish frontier, and the tsar's coolness and suspicion. Instead of patiently continuing to sooth their ruffled feelings he allowed himself some show of resentment through his controlled press and a mounting campaign against Russian credit, culminating in the decision on 10 November 1887 that the Reichsbank should not in future accept Russian bonds as security for loans. Bismarck's interview with the tsar in Berlin on 18 November did nothing, in the circumstances, to improve relations, particularly as the tsar had recently seen letters (undoubtedly forged) which suggested that Bismarck was secretly backing Ferdinand's candidacy.

In the meantime Bismarck encouraged the Mediterranean group to tighten their links. A new Italian prime minister, Francesco Crispi, enthusiastically contemplating a vigorous and expansive foreign policy, readily agreed with Bismarck on 2 and 3 October that Russia must not have Constantinople (**11**). Salisbury, while accepting the fact that Germany's contribution would be mainly to keep France quiet, nevertheless professed doubts about the future of German policy, and received a long and reassuring private letter from Bismarck on 22 November (**12**). The second group of Mediterranean agreements, pledging Britain, Austria, and Italy to maintain the *status quo* in the East, was then concluded on 12 December 1887. The tsar probably had some inkling by this stage of the grouping against him and the Bulgarian crisis ended when he decided to be satisfied with the Porte's declaration on 4 March 1888 as to the illegality of Ferdinand's accession. Bismarck supported Russia on this point at Constantinople, although he was unable to persuade Kálnoky to do so (**13**).

1 A French Anticipation of revived German Hostility

M. Raindre (chargé d'affaires, Berlin) to Freycinet, 6 August 1885

[The acrimonious article of 3 August directed against France by the *Norddeutsche Allgemeine Zeitung* denouncing the excesses of French chauvinism] has naturally caused a stir in the political world of Berlin, and roused a great deal of curiosity.

. . . I do not believe that the demonstration of malevolence directed against our country has its chief origin in the preoccupations of domestic politics, and, as I have indicated in a recent telegram, I would be more inclined to believe it was dictated by considerations connected with the situation abroad. . . . The Gladstone ministry had given way to the cabinet of Salisbury and the Chancellor found in this change, with the satisfaction of his personal antipathies, general guarantees of goodwill and conciliation on the part of the British government. And so from that time on he became for us, in the questions still unresolved and in which we are more directly engaged than Germany, a more exacting ally, more difficult to keep.

DDF, I, vi (*bis*), no. 2

2   The Bulgarian Unification Crisis: Bismarck reins in Austria

(i) *Malet to Salisbury, despatch no. 435, 22 September 1885*

I asked Prince Bismarck today whether Germany or Austria took the lead in deciding questions of policy regarding the East. He replied that he left all minor questions to Austria, giving her free swing as long as the tranquillity of Europe was not endangered, but that if he saw that she was moving too quickly or without sufficiently foreseeing the consequences he took the reins into his own hand and was able to hold them. . . .

F.O. 64/1079

(ii) *Bismarck to Reusz, despatch no. 561, 3 October 1885*

. . . The union of Bulgaria and Eastern Rumelia is not yet a fait accompli, and maybe never will be; for the *personal* union suggested by England and not rejected by M. Giers, i.e. the appointment of Prince Battenberg as Turkish governor of Eastern Rumelia, would not mean the restoration of Greater Bulgaria. If, as I hope, Austria also advocates this combination, then I think that success is very probable.

Count Kálnoky spoke to Y.E. of '*obligations*' of Austria to Serbia, and must have had in mind the treaty of friendship which was concluded in the year 1880[3] with Serbia, before the present agreement with Russia, in M. Haymerle's time.... By this treaty Serbia had linked herself with Austrian policy for ten years; moreover the treaty was of a defensive character without any territorial guarantees.

Austria is not obliged to hasten to Serbia's aid, if the latter involves herself in war by unilateral aggression, and we should be sorry to see Austria taking over the responsibility for the excesses of Serbian policy without being able to guide and control the latter. The statement that Austria will not leave Serbia in the lurch possesses, because of what King Milan by virtue of his temperament will read into it, a dangerous significance which worries me. The obligation of Austria to support the Obrenovic dynasty involves a reciprocal duty on the part of the King not to divorce himself from Austrian policy, and Count Kálnoky himself admits that Austria will leave Serbia to its fate, if the latter tries to achieve the desired compensations otherwise than by intervention of the powers. It is true that the banishment of the King and his replacement by Karageorgevic, Ristic or some other adventurer, would be just as unwelcome to us as to Austria; but I will not admit that Austria, faced with two evils, would choose the lesser, if its policy of keeping Milan on the throne were to lead to a war with Russia.

To encourage the presumption of the small Balkan states, which only originated with the Berlin Congress, is in my opinion dangerous; it has no definite bounds, and if similarly excited Serbian ambition might, under different circumstances, turn against Austria with talk of a Serbia irredenta in the Banat unless one keeps reminding these ambitious states that if the treaty of Berlin is destroyed they will also lose the *rights* which they gained by it.

There is no question of Serbia's *right* to compensation if Bulgaria and Eastern Rumelia become united, in whatever sense one construes 'right'; the supposed justification, preservation of the balance of power, will not stand up to examination.... Your Ex. has rightly remarked that any compensation for Serbia would only whet the appetite of the other Balkan states. ...

GP, v, no. 958

(iii) *Salisbury to Malet, despatch no. 489, 5 November 1885*

[Thinks that the German Government have not rightly apprehended the British Government's line of thought with regard to the restoration

---

[3] Bismarck is in error here: the Austro-Serbian treaty was signed on 28 June 1881, ten days after the signature of the Three Emperors' Alliance treaty.

of the *status quo* in Eastern Rumelia.] At the outset, Her Majesty's Government are confronted with the difficulty that they cannot, as members of a Conference, be consenting or sanctioning Parties to the suppression, by military force, of an insurgent population in a foreign country. This rule of conduct is independent of the opinion they may form on the merits of the intervention. There may in a conceivable case be no objection to urge to a policy of repression; such a course of action may even be quite right. But it is none the less against the traditional policy of Great Britain that the Queen's Government should take part in controversies between the Sovereign and the subjects of another country to the extent which I have mentioned. . . .

F.O. 64/1075

(iv) *Kálnoky to Khevenhüller (Nish), telegram no. 81, 14 November 1885*

In view of the continuing delays in the conference and the untenable position of the Serbian army drawn up on the frontier, we could not be surprised at the decision of the king to march in. We believe that it was of considerable advantage to Serbia to have been on legal ground during the meeting of the Delegations, inasmuch as the sympathetic demonstrations during the course of it imply a significant strengthening of her position. We wish Serbia all success, and have already been preparing the way for this event with the other powers during the last few weeks. . . .

WSA, XV(85)

(v) *Wolkenstein (St. Petersburg) to Kálnoky, telegram no. 188, 1 December 1885*

[Giers on Khevenhüller: spoke to me in an excited manner.] The latter had indicated to Prince Alexander as emergency measures if the hostilities continued 1. the entry of Austrian troops into Serbia and 2. the invasion of Bulgaria by Russia. The former might be accepted by Giers; the latter was, however, quite inadmissible, as it would be demanding a moral impossibility from Russia. This news put the Emperor Alexander in a bad mood, and he had charged Giers to discuss it with me. Referring to the official information sent to me, I replied that I had only learned of point 1 through a quite unauthorized press telegram, but knew of point 2 through a communication from Giers. In any case it was to be assumed that Count Khevenhüller's language was grave and pungent, but it had to be in order to achieve what Russia was striving for—namely cessation of hostilities. There was, however, no proof that the emergency measures denounced by Giers had really been taken. The Bulgars had every reason to pretend that they were under the strongest diplomatic pressure from several great powers and so their statements were suspect. . . .

WSA, XV(80)

(vi) *H. von Bismarck to Reusz, unsigned draft, 7 December 1885*

Secret.

From confidential communications received from Count Hatzfeldt we can assume with certainty that the English ministers adopt the principle that they need not trouble about English interests in the east, as Austria will and must fight them out alone. The Chancellor finds that the rash and precipitate zeal with which the Austrian government is proceeding to get the matter in train and draw Russian hostility will give the English cabinet every cause to assume that Austria will proceed to act alone; in this case England would let Austria exhaust herself, then in accordance with the Gladstone programme come to an understanding with Russia at the expense of Austria.

These English reports confirm how very right the Chancellor was to warn Austria against any excitable policy which it has followed recently to his regret. If Austria could curb her impatience and be guided in her policy by statesmanlike considerations, she could safeguard her interests if Russia were *already* at war with England or simply in possession of Constantinople. The English need in their own estimation about two more years, before they will be unassailable in India; until then they will seek to avoid all conflict with Russia. Lord Salisbury told Count Hatzfeldt that if the Turks really invaded Eastern Rumelia England would naturally hold to her point of view and reserve the right to advise; but naturally she will not mobilize a single man to prevent it. Russia needs perhaps less than two years to prepare for an offensive; if Austrian policy has not the courage to wait for it, then the Chancellor declared that he could not give Austria any help.

Prince Bismarck asks Y.E. to speak confidentially to Count Kálnoky in the foregoing sense, but to regard this despatch as strictly secret, and in particular the reference to a possible occupation of Constantinople by Russia.

GP, iv, no. 861

3   Growing Russian Exasperation over Bulgaria

Wolkenstein to Kálnoky, telegram no. 130, 4 October 1886

Confidential. Y.E.'s telegrams to no. 171 received.

M. Giers is disturbed by the latest Bulgarian reports. He calls the present journey [by General Kaulbars] the culminating point. Speeches of M. Tisza will have helped to encourage Bulgarian resistance. According to Giers the cabinet of St. Petersburg should have limited itself to telling the Austro-Hungarian and German governments that it was not considering occupation, but it should never have divulged this intention, particularly not in Bulgaria. ... To me M. de Giers has vigorously insisted that the Russian government was only seeking a means of getting out of the very difficult situation confronting it in Bulgaria.

WSA, Rapp. de St. Petersbourg 1886

4   Bismarck advises Robilant to prefer a British to a French Alliance

Count von Rantzau (Varzin), memorandum for Herbert Bismarck, 16 October 1886

Secret.

The Chancellor thanks Count Robilant through Count Launay for his communication, and adds that he will treat it as secret in accordance with the Minister's wishes. First of all he could wish that Italy, if she has to choose between us and France, would attach herself to us and Austria. The promise about Tripoli sought by Italy might be discussed; we would have no decided objection, especially if Austria should agree. But if, as in the Mediterranean question, it were a matter of Italy's choosing between France and England, it would seem to His Highness that of the two, England would be the less dangerous ally for Italy. An Italian alliance with France, which succeeded in paralysing England, would finally leave France and Italy alone as rival neighbours, France's aim being then to achieve, as in the time of the last empire, supremacy over Italy. Relying on Count Robilant's good sense, and his obvious aversion to such an alliance, His Highness also believes that it is in our interest as well as Italy's not to agree to it.

His Highness requests that the Count should be spoken to confidentially in this sense.

GP, iv, no. 827

5   Bismarck's Speech of 11 January 1887

[Addressing the German Reichstag, Bismarck, after quoting Hamlet's remark, 'What's Hecuba to him?' continued:] What's Bulgaria to us? It is a matter of complete indifference to us who rules in Bulgaria, and what becomes of Bulgaria—and that I repeat. I repeat everything that I said earlier when I used that expression, so much misused and ridden to death since, about the bones of a Pomeranian grenadier:[4] in the whole Eastern question there is no question of war for us. No one is going to embroil us with Russia. (Bravo on the right.) Russia's friendship means more to us than that of Bulgaria and all the friends of Bulgaria that we have with us in this country. (Laughter on the right.)

The question as to how we shall stand with France in the future, I find less easy to answer . . . is this epoch of frontier warfare with the French nation at an end, or is it not? You are as little able to answer that question as I am. I can only voice my own suspicions in this regard, and say that it is not at an end; this would need a change in the entire French character and the whole frontier situation.

On our side we have done everything to persuade the French to forget the past. . . .

GW, xiii, pp. 212-13

6   Bismarck's Terms for Anglo-German Cooperation

Bismarck to Hatzfeldt, despatch no. 98, 3 February 1887

[He has had a long conversation with the English ambassador]. I made it clear to Sir Edward Malet that in the present situation we could do little more than hold France in check. But if this is done, in the full sense of the word, it will allow England as well as Italy greater freedom of movement, and if these two powers in combination with Austria are seemingly strong enough to prevent Russia from disturbing the peace, and if on the other hand Germany and France so counterbalance each other that one sword keeps the other in its scabbard, then equilibrium and peace in Europe would be assured. Both depend solely on England; but if England withdraws from that combination, then we should be forced to seek other expedients already mentioned, in order to do what we can on our side for the maintenance of peace.

[4] Cf. B, 3: the musketeer has now become a grenadier.

I repeatedly assured the English ambassador that we should not attack France in spite of all Boulangist provocation, and with reference to the English press posed the question, whether England really believes it is in her interest to see war break out between us and France. Several English newspapers seemed to suggest that it was, but I cannot believe it. Sir Edward Malet also denied it vehemently and assured me that England could not want war in itself, and still less a defeat of Germany in such a war, because England would then find herself alone with France and Russia on the European scene. This assumption is correct, but if England thinks she can sit back and leave us to settle alone all questions on the continent, then there is always the danger that one day, even without the downfall of Germany, she may find herself having to face one of the continental powers in isolation, simply because of her refusal to take part in European politics. In the interest of Germany's safety I consider it expedient to seek a rapprochement either with England or Russia, if peace and equilibrium cannot be assured by the constellation I have sketched above.

The foregoing is not meant to be a commission for Y.E. to make overtures to Lord Salisbury, but merely for your own information and as a guide for use if occasion arises. I assume that Sir Edward Malet will have reported to Lord Salisbury yesterday on the lines of my conversation with him.

GP, iv, no. 883

7   Treaty between Germany and Italy, 20 February 1887

[Preamble states that this treaty supplements the treaty of alliance concluded on 20 May 1882, and renewed this day.]

Article I. The high Contracting Parties, having in mind only the maintenance, so far as possible, of the territorial *status quo* in the East, engage to use their influence to forestall, on the Ottoman coasts and islands in the Adriatic and the Aegean Seas, any territorial modification which might be injurious to one or the other of the Powers signatory to the present treaty. To this end they shall communicate to one another all information of a nature to enlighten each other mutually concerning their own dispositions, as well as those of other Powers.

Article II. The stipulations of Article I apply in no way to the Egyptian question, with regard to which the High Contracting Parties preserve respectively their freedom of action, regard being always paid to the principles upon which rest the present treaty and that of May 1882.

Article III. If it were to happen that France should make a move to extend her occupation, or even her protectorate or her sovereignty, under any form whatsoever, in the North African territories, whether of the Vilayet of Tripoli or of the Moroccan Empire, and that in consequence thereof Italy, in order to safeguard her position in the Mediterranean, should feel that she must herself undertake action in the said North African territories, or even have recourse to extreme measures in French territory in Europe, the state of war which would thereby ensue between Italy and France would constitute *ipso facto*, on the demand of Italy and at the common charge of the two Allies, the *casus foederis* with all the effects foreseen by Articles II and V of the aforesaid treaty of 20 May 1882, as if such an eventuality were expressly contemplated therein.

Article IV. If the fortunes of any war undertaken in common against France should lead Italy to seek for territorial guarantees with respect to France for the security of the frontiers of the Kingdom and of her maritime position, as well as with a view to the stability of peace, Germany will present no obstacle thereto; and, if need be, and in a measure compatible with circumstances, will apply herself to facilitating the means of attaining such a purpose.

[Articles V, VI, and VII provide for secrecy and ratification.]

Pribram, i, 111–15

8   The Schnaebele Incident

Memorandum by Herbert von Bismarck, 24 April 1887

The French ambassador handed me today the attached documents remarking that from them could be concluded without any doubt that Schnäbele had been taken prisoner on French soil.[5] I replied that our reports hitherto had been to the contrary: but I would carefully study the enclosures and compare them with the statement which I expected from the chief public prosecutor and the examining magistrate.

[5] (Marginal note by Bismarck:) The main difficulty in the situation lies in the fact that Schnebele was seized while attending an *official* conference on the question of international boundaries. Such conferences are in the same category as meetings with enemy officers with flags of truce, and must guarantee safe conduct, otherwise official border conferences will be impossible.

Hitherto we had only had short reports from police officers, and I must therefore postpone any further discussion and definitive statement until I had had the official report. Should it transpire from this that Schnäbele had actually been seized on the other side of the boundary-post, then he would be set at liberty again. . . .

GP, vi, no. 1262

9   The Reinsurance Treaty, 18 June 1887

Article I. If one of the high contracting Parties should find itself at war with a third Great Power, the other would maintain a benevolent neutrality, and would try to localize the conflict. This provision would not apply to a war against Austria or France resulting from an attack on one of these two Powers by one of the high contracting Parties.

Article II. Germany recognizes the rights historically acquired by Russia in the Balkan peninsula, and particularly the legitimacy of her preponderant and decisive influence in Bulgaria and in Eastern Roumelia. The two Courts engage to admit no modification of the territorial status quo of the said peninsula without a previous agreement between them, and to oppose in due course every attempt to disturb this status quo, or to modify it without their consent.

Article III. The two Courts recognize the European and mutually obligatory character of the principle of the closing of the Straits of the Bosphorus and of the Dardanelles, founded on international law, confirmed by the treaties and summed up in the declaration of the Second Plenipotentiary of Russia at the session of 12 July of the Congress of Berlin (protocol 19).

They will ensure in common that Turkey shall make no exception to this rule in favour of the interests of any Government whatsoever, by lending to the warlike operations of a belligerent Power the portion of its Empire which forms the Straits. In case of infringement, or to prevent it if such infringement should be in prospect, the two Courts will inform Turkey that they would regard her, in this event, as putting herself in a state of war towards the injured party, and as depriving herself thenceforth of the benefits of the security assured to her territorial status quo by the Treaty of Berlin.

Article IV. The present Treaty shall remain in force for the space of three years from the day of the exchange of ratifications.

[Articles V, VI—provision for secrecy and ratification.]

ADDITIONAL AND VERY SECRET PROTOCOL, 18 JUNE 1887

In order to complete the stipulations of Articles II and III of the secret treaty concluded on the same date, the two Courts are agreed on the following points:

1. Germany, as in the past, will lend Russia a free hand in order to re-establish a regular and legal Government in Bulgaria.—She promises not to give in any case Her consent to the restoration of the Prince of Battenberg.

2. If His Majesty the Emperor of Russia should find Himself under the necessity of assuming the task of defending the entrance of the Black Sea in order to safeguard the interests of Russia, Germany undertakes to accord Her benevolent neutrality and Her moral and diplomatic support to the measures which His Majesty may deem it necessary to take to guard the key of His Empire.

3. [Protocol has same validity as main treaty.]

(L.S.) BISMARCK
(L.S.) PAUL SCHOUVALOF

GP, v, 253-5

10   Kálnoky on the Contradictions in German Policy

Kálnoky to Calice, private letter, 18 August 1887

... What does us most harm at the moment in the east is the attitude of Germany in the Bulgarian question. It is quite true, and Prince Reusz has confirmed this, that Prince Bismarck, faithful to his earlier attitude, supports the Russian plans concerning Bulgaria on Constantinople and has advised the Sultan to come to an understanding with Russia, that is, to lead the Russians back to Bulgaria. This does not surprise me, and I was convinced that Bismarck will not change his russophile attitude as far as Bulgaria is concerned. On the other hand I doubt whether he will do more than remain consistent in theory, but this is more than enough to jeopardize the influence of our group. It is not to be wondered at if this peculiar attitude of Germany *vis-à-vis* the Sultan is misunderstood and causes confusion and distrust. Only a short while ago Germany sided with us, Italy, and England against the action of France and Russia in the Egyptian question. A few weeks later Germany, together with France, supports the Russians in a course of action which is blatantly hostile to us. What will the Turks make of this, and is it to be wondered at if they conclude that reliable alliances are no longer to be had? And yet it would not be true to believe that our alliance with Germany has in any way been undermined—on the contrary, on the German side there is an even greater effort to foster and cherish this alliance as the only reliable prop and bastion against war and its advocates. . . . It must be because of the very vulnerable position of Germany between France and Russia that Bismarck keeps trying to separate Russia from France by showing favour to the Emperor Alexander in the Bulgarian question, in which he has such a personal interest. . . .

WSA, Mittelmeerabkommen Liasse 1887

11 Crispi's Confidence in Bismarck's Attitude

Bruck (Rome) to Kálnoky, private letter, 15 October 1887

[Crispi made the following remarks to Bruck in conversation.] Believe me, I am completely at your service, and if as a result of circumstances which could arise at any moment you were to say to me: On such and such a day we will have one or two hundred thousand men at such and such a place; then all right, you will find there one or two hundred thousand Italians who will be at your disposal and you can do what you like with them. United you and we can defeat Russia, and Turkey at the same time if necessary—As to France, that is not our concern, for Bismarck has told me that it is his affair and that he will take care of them. And as for Poland, take it and put an archduke in as sovereign, they will ask nothing more and you will be the gainer. Prince Bismarck shares my point of view, and I can assure you he has had enough of Russia. . . .

WSA, Mittelmeerabkommen Liasse 1887

12 Bismarck defines the permanent Realities of German foreign policy

Bismarck to Salisbury, private letter, 22 November 1887

[Writes to offer an exchange of ideas which may prove useful to both Germany and England in view of England's interest in the Austro-Italian entente. Starts by dealing with Salisbury's suggestion that

Prince William, if he came to the throne, might follow a pro-Russian policy: all German rulers must follow a rigorous path dictated by German interests, and the army in particular, recruited from all classes of the population, was a guarantee that Germany would fight only to defend national independence and the integrity of the Empire.] ... Austria, as well as Germany and the England of today, belongs to the number of satisfied nations, 'saturated' in the words of the late Prince Metternich, and hence pacific and conservative. Austria and England have loyally accepted the *status quo* of the German empire, and have no interest in seeing it weakened. France and Russia on the other hand seem to be threatening us: France by remaining true to the traditions of past centuries which show her to be the constant enemy of her neighbours and hence a part of the French national character; Russia by adopting today *vis-à-vis* Europe the attitude, disquieting for European peace, which characterized France during the reigns of Louis XIV and Napoleon I. ...

Given this state of affairs we must regard as permanent the danger that our peace will be disturbed by France and Russia. Our policy therefore will necessarily tend to secure what alliances we can in view of the possibility of having to fight our two powerful neighbours simultaneously. If the alliance between friendly powers threatened by the *same* belligerent nations were not forthcoming our situation in a war on both fronts would not be a matter for despair; but war against France and Russia allied, even supposing that as a military exploit its end should be as glorious for us as the Seven Years War, would always be a sufficiently great calamity for our country for us to try and avoid it by an amicable arrangement with Russia, if we had to do it *without* an ally. But as long as we are not sure of being forsaken by powers whose interests are identical with ours, no Emperor of Germany can follow any other line of policy than that of defending the independence of friendly powers, satisfied as we are with the present state of Europe and ready to act without hesitation or weakness when their independence is threatened. Thus we shall avoid a Russian war as long as this is compatible with our honour and security, and as long as the independence of Austria-Hungary, whose existence as a great power is of paramount importance for us, is not called into question. We hope that the friendly powers who have interests to safeguard in the east which we do not share will, both by alliance and military force, become strong enough to keep Russia's sword in its scabbard, or to resist, if circumstances lead to a rupture. As long as German interests are not involved, we shall remain neutral; but it is impossible to concede that the German Emperor could ever lend the *support* of his arms to Russia to aid her in vanquishing or weakening one of the powers on whose support we are counting, whether in order to avoid a Russian war, or to aid us in facing her. From this point of view Germany would *always* be obliged to enter the fighting line if the independence of Austria-Hungary were threatened by Russian aggression, or if England or Italy ran the risk of being invaded by the French. German policy will therefore follow a course forcibly prescribed by the political situation in Europe, and from which the antipathies or the sympathies of neither a particular monarch nor a responsible minister will make her deviate. . . .

GP, iv, no. 930

13   Bismarck recommends a Final Conciliatory Gesture by Austria

Széchényi to Kálnoky, telegram no. 25, 19 February 1888

The Chancellor has asked me through Count Herbert Bismarck to beg Y.E. not to make the discussion of what would happen regarding Bulgaria in the event of Prince Ferdinand's refusal a precondition for the acceptance of the Russian refusal. The Emperor Alexander would inevitably look upon this as a *fin de non recevoir* (act of obstruction) from us, and consider our refusal as a disguised wish to keep the Prince of Coburg in Bulgaria, and this would feed the Emperor's wrath, inasmuch as his demand not only lies within the framework of the Berlin treaty, but is directed against a violation of it. Here, too, the Russian proposal is not regarded as a practical expedient, but the Emperor Alexander thinks it is, because he is convinced that a collective step taken by the powers must bring about the retreat of Prince Ferdinand. Possibly this would not happen, but it is of great importance for us that they should not be able to say in St. Petersburg that our refusal had brought it about, and had even led other powers to follow suit in refusing. To my argument, taken from your despatch of 16th inst, I was given the reply that Y.E. was requested to see in the matter under discussion only a question of the dignity and *amour propre* of the Emperor Alexander. It has cost enough effort to bring him to the point of making any proposal at all, and it would be a pity to miss this opportunity of being in close touch with him again. Accordingly there is the liveliest desire here that, if Y.E. cannot avoid introducing a discussion of what the consequences might be, it should be done at most in the form of an additional expectation, and not as a condition. And finally I would add that the Russian proposal has already been communicated to Rome, and found support there.

WSA, Bulgarien-Frage 1888

J

THE LAST PHASE, 1888-1898

Bismarck resigned—being virtually dismissed by Emperor William II—on 20 March 1890. Foreign affairs during the last two years of his chancellorship were, as far as the public could judge, uneventful, and it was believed that the quarrel between the two men was primarily over domestic policy. Each in fact possessed an over-developed will to dominate government; compromise was impossible, and both domestic and foreign issues contributed to the breach. Bismarck was unquestionably uneasy about Germany's place in the diplomatic alignments; and he had no confidence in the ability of the young emperor or the new advisers to solve problems which he could not solve himself.

Throughout 1888 the Russian and French governments showed continued resentment over Germany's bearing during the 1887 crises, and little inclination to be overawed by Bismarck's formidable displays of irritability. The tsar remained distrustful, but accepted the logic of Giers' argument that Russia had much more to lose than to gain by a breach with Germany. Bismarck's speech of 6 February 1888, emphasizing desire for good relations with Russia and justifying the Austrian alliance as a strictly defensive measure, reiterated Germany's sturdy but peaceful disposition in a noble peroration (1); it so encouraged Giers as to lead him to seek Bismarck's support for the Porte's declaration of the illegality of Prince Ferdinand's position in Bulgaria (cf. p. 154). The tsar still found Boulangism and its repercussions in France distasteful. It was believed that Germany alone held back Austria and her friends from aggressive action in the Balkans; the Russians were unaware of the extent to which Bismarck had instigated the defensive grouping against them, but were also unaware of the thoroughness with which he deprecated talk of a preventive war against Russia (favoured by the young emperor before his accession, by Count Waldersee, the Quartermaster-General, and other soldiers, and by Holstein and others in the foreign office).[1] However, the continued war on Russian credit, which was leading to a major financial *rapprochement* between Russia and France, kept Russian mistrust alive.

Bismarck protested strongly in April 1888 against the Empress Frederick's plan to marry her daughter Victoria to Prince Alexander of Battenberg. He thought it would infuriate the tsar, who, however, to Bismarck's annoyance, did not appear to take the matter too tragically. Bismarck turned angrily

[1] Norman Rich, *Friedrich von Holstein* (Cambridge, 1965), i, 216-20

against Queen Victoria, whose complicity he suspected, and launched a campaign in the German press (2), but at a meeting between these two impressive personalities in Berlin on 25 April he explained his desire for peace and fears of Russia and France in terms which secured her cordial approval. The tsar was in fact pleased that the Battenberg marriage project was dropped.

It was France rather than Russia whose initiative in 1888 revealed the inadequacies of the Bismarckian system. The French had no intention of getting into a shooting war with Italy, but they conducted ruthlessly a tariff war in which Crispi had involved his unfortunate country. In December 1886 Crispi's predecessors had denounced the Franco-Italian commercial treaty of 1881, although France normally took as much as thirty per cent of Italian exports. Crispi's efforts during 1887 to negotiate a new treaty with more favourable tariff terms were defeated both by the French protectionist urge to do the same for themselves and by Crispi's ostentatious courting of Bismarck in October 1887. There was nothing to encourage the French ministers to throw away their strongest bargaining weapon. Italian exports and credit were badly hit, there was widespread distress (particularly in the south), and it soon became evident in 1888 that France was better fitted than Italy to stand a tariff war of these proportions.

Bismarck chose to interpret French action in political terms, and to redouble his efforts to protect the Italian and German positions against a possible French attack. This policy was probably misconceived and certainly ineffectual. It is true that Boulangism continued to cause alarm until the general's flight to Brussels in April 1889, but the chances (if they ever existed) of a French decision for war even against Italy had passed with Rouvier's appointment in May 1887. The evidence is against the view that Bismarck was seeking to provoke France into war, but it suggests that he encouraged Crispi's flamboyant gestures in order to overawe the French and in order to stampede the British into full association with the Triple Alliance. For his part Crispi may have wished—as the French believed—to provoke war when he was certain of success with the aid of the Triple Alliance, but more probably was seeking to wave the flag and force French concessions over the colonial and tariff issues. A military agreement of January 1888 for the sending of Italian troops to the Rhineland in the event of war can be interpreted in either sense.

Britain's main value lay in her navy, which alone could counter France's powerful naval forces in the Mediterranean and protect Italy's vulnerable coastline. Periodically, Crispi, as in February and March 1888, showed alarm, which Bismarck seemed genuinely to share, as to a French naval assault. Salisbury was prepared to promise immediate help by the British navy in such a case, but, increasingly distrustful of Crispi after the spring of 1888, did not intend to commit himself beyond the 1887 agreements (3). Yet it is evident that in Bismarck's eyes Britain was now the decisive factor in the European situation; if she could be brought into full collaboration with the Triple Alliance the balance would be firmly tilted against the potential aggressors, France and Russia.

In short, the Three Emperors' Alliance, the centrepiece of the Bismarckian system from 1873 to 1887, was shattered, and the alternative system of the Triple Alliance was not convincing. Bismarck's unsuccessful attempt at the very end of his career to construct a new alliance system based on British reinforcement is evidence in some measure of overall failure, even if German power and authority remained great. The attempt to woo Britain was seen in various public protestations of friendship (5), in an accommodating turn to German colonial policy resulting in the Anglo-German treaty of 1 July 1890 (concluded after Bismarck's dismissal), and in a specific offer of alliance in January 1889.

Bismarck's anxiety to retain Italian friendship while avoiding war on her behalf led, on the one hand, to a zealous encouragement of Crispi's pretensions, and, on the other, to efforts to bring the British navy more actively into the picture. In recent years British naval power was considered to have declined, technically and even numerically, by comparison with the French, and there was some doubt as to whether Britain could now, in view of her commitments in the Channel, the Atlantic, and the Far East, match the powerful French Mediterranean force based on Toulon. Bismarck in a personal message to Salisbury through Hatzfeldt in January 1889 suggested a defensive alliance between the two countries for one, two, or three years: he argued that England had, apart from France, divergent interests with the United States and Russia, but a war with one or even both these two would be a mortal danger to her only if France joined them. So Bismarck would undertake to keep France quiet while Britain hastened her naval rearmament. He preferred a public treaty, ratified by the two parliaments; publicity would deter, and in any case he no doubt understood Salisbury's inability to sign a formal secret treaty (4). A few days later, on 26 January 1889, he spoke warmly in the Reichstag of Britain as a virtual ally (5).

Salisbury took time to consult his colleagues, and spoke to Herbert Bismarck in March of the beneficial features of the plan, but said that the time was inopportune, for it did not appear that the proposal would be acceptable to the government's parliamentary following. This was undoubtedly true. But it is also evident that Salisbury distrusted Crispi, saw no need for an irrevocable breach with the calculating Frenchmen, and did not trust the German leaders sufficiently to commit himself irrevocably to an Anglo-German alliance. He found safety in the naval defence act of March 1889, which introduced the two-power standard.

Bismarck's system for Europe depended too much upon the willingness of other politicians, in Germany and abroad, to promote his peace of mind. At home, he alone, backed by the old emperor, could hold power—an exasperating situation for rival politicians, even if they accepted the broad aims of his policy. The young emperor William and his entourage quickly decided that they wanted to change the pilot, and soon the course, of the ship of state. Abroad, the system involved a curious balancing of antagonisms—other European states must remain sufficiently antagonistic to checkmate one another, but not sufficiently so to be driven to fight.

In his somewhat embittered retirement he tended to justify the prolongation of this frustrating situation as evidence of Germany's peaceful intentions and his own skill and moderation. Yet he could fairly claim to have played a large part in mobilizing the conservative forces in Europe in defence of peace on Germany's own terms until the point at which a new dynamism in politics, which was bound ultimately to revolutionize the foreign policy of his own country, swept him out of office. His control was weakening because he was neither able nor willing to dominate and direct these forces, as he had after all directed them before 1871.[2] On the other hand, his system had not collapsed: the supreme crisis of choice for him would arise only in the event of a final Russo-Austrian breach, and after the collapse of the Three Emperors' Alliance he had postponed this choice by his separate treaties with the other two. It is the considered view of some German historians that in the last resort and in order to avoid a two-front war he would have thrown over Austria in order to purchase Russian neutrality.[3] But as a result of the chancellor's own expedients this issue was not put to the test.

We close with two extracts illustrating the vein in which he brooded over and vindicated the all-sufficiency of his own tactics and policy during his last years (6, 7). His *Reflections and Reminiscences*, published after his death in 1898, is remarkable for its wide range (although essentially episodic in treatment), weighty judgments, and imperviousness to viewpoints other than his own.

1   Bismarck's Reichstag Speech of 6 February 1888

[In the debate in the Reichstag on a new army bill Bismarck, after surveying his efforts to assist Russia at the Congress of Berlin, went on to justify the treaty with Austria, the text of which had been published on 3 February 1888, as a purely defensive measure.

... After continuing in this vein for some time, Bismarck concluded his speech as follows.] And so I can declare that the ill-feeling which has been voiced against us by Russian public opinion and particularly in the Russian press will not deter us from supporting any diplomatic steps which Russia can take to win back her influence on Bulgaria, as soon as Russia makes her wishes known. ... I do not doubt that the Emperor of Russia, when he finds that the interests of his large empire of 100 million subjects demand that he makes war, will do so. But his interests cannot possibly require him to make this war on us, and I do not think there is any imminent danger of this happening.

---

[2] H. Krausnick, *Holsteins Geheimpolitik in der Ära Bismarck*, 1886-1890 (Hamburg, 1942), pp. 157-68.

[3] G. Ritter, *Lebendige Vergangenheit*, pp. 121-2; W. Mommsen, *Bismarck*, p. 190.

If I may sum up, I do not think there is any imminent threat to peace and I beg that you will give consideration to the law now laid before you quite independently of this thought and fear, and merely as a full restoration of the use of the great power that God has vested in the German nation for use in time of need; if we do not need it, we shall not call upon it; we are seeking to avoid the necessity for using it.

But this effort of ours is being made somewhat difficult by the threatening articles in foreign newspapers, and I would like to exhort these foreign countries in particular to cease these threats. They will achieve nothing. The threats being directed against us—not by the government—but by the press, are incredibly stupid (laughter), if they think that they can intimidate a great and proud power like the German empire by a threatening array of printer's ink and an assemblage of words. (Bravo!) They should cease this activity, and then it would be easier for us to have more pleasant relations with our neighbours. Every country is in the long run answerable at some time for the windows broken by its press: and some day the account is presented in the form of the ill-humour of the other country. We may easily— perhaps too easily—be bribed by love and goodwill, but definitely not by threats! (Bravo!) We Germans fear God, and nothing else on earth (loud shouts of Bravo!); and it is the fear of God which makes us love and cherish peace. But whoever violates peace will realize that the war- like patriotism, which in 1813 called the whole population of the then tiny, weak and impoverished Prussia to the colours, is now a common attribute of the whole German nation, and that he who attacks the German nation in any way will find them armed and united, and every soldier with the firm belief in his heart, 'God will be on our side'. (Loud and long applause, during which Count Moltke goes up to the Chancellor and congratulates him on his speech.) . . .

GW, xiii, 341, 346-7

2 Salisbury on the Battenberg Marriage crisis

Salisbury to Queen Victoria, telegram, 8 April 1888

I have received several private telegrams from Sir E. Malet, showing that Prince Bismarck is in one of his raging moods about the proposed marriage.

He shows temper against Your Majesty and as at such times he is quite unscrupulous, he will probably try to give currency to statements which are designed to make Your Majesty personally responsible for any evil results of his own violent passion.... The newspapers say that Your Majesty is going to Potsdam or Berlin. I would humbly submit that this visit at this time would expose You to great misconstruction and possibly to some disrespectful demonstration.

German Chancellor is reported by his son to be in a state of intense exasperation, drinking stimulants all day and narcotics by night.

F. Ponsonby, *Letters of the Empress Frederick* (London, 1928), p. 295

3 Growing British reserve towards Crispi's foreign policy

Salisbury to Dufferin, 28 December 1888

... The armed peace is leading Italy rapidly to financial ruin. If there could be war Crispi hopes for Albania certainly, Nice probably and perhaps Tunis and Tripoli. (There is some promise of the first two Herbert Bismarck hints.) If there is to be war at all, it is to Italy's interest to have it as quickly as possible. (Both Blanc and Damiani [head of the Italian foreign office] said so.)

The consequence has been a string of quarrels with France.... Under these circumstances our policy has altered a little—not much. At first we were very cordial with Italy—which is our normal policy. But as Crispi's character developed we came to the conclusion that it was better to give him a wide berth.

We have therefore kept out of his quarrels with France and declined to give any guarantees beyond a strong desire for the *status quo* in the Mediterranean. My impression is that if France attacked Italy gratuitously by sea, the English feeling would be in favour of going to her assistance, but that if a war were to arise out of one of Crispi's trumpery quarrels, England would certainly stand aloof. I confess I should be very glad to see Crispi disappear—spite of the German fondness for him. His conspirator's temper (he was one of Garibaldi's hundred) leads him to political gambling, which, in the present state of men's feelings, is full of danger to the world's peace. I am glad to think that the financial mess into which he has got will help to bring about that consummation. The Germans indeed tell me now that it is Damiani who is the firebrand and that he pushes Crispi. This suggestion, even

if it were true, makes little difference, because no one else but Crispi
would be pushed by Damiani.

Salisbury Papers: Cecil, iv, 105;
C. J. Lowe, *The Reluctant
Imperialists*, ii, 83

4 Bismarck's alliance offer to England, January 1889

Bismarck to Hatzfeldt, 11 January 1889

No. 31.
[During a recent visit to Friedrichsruh, Hatzfeldt was instructed to take
the earliest opportunity to discuss with Salisbury the possibility of a
public treaty as a guarantee of peace.]
England and Germany are not threatened by attack other than from
the French. Only in the event of Austro-Russian entanglements could
Germany be drawn into a war with Russia, and as the latter, even in
the most propitious circumstances, could offer no acceptable fruits of
war, we must use all our endeavours to avoid an Austrian war as far as
possible.

The only threat to the two friendly powers, Germany and England,
is France, the neighbour of both; they have no other common neighbour which constitutes a threat. England has a clash of interests not only
with France, but also with North America and Russia. But a war with
one of *these* two, even a simultaneous war with both, will only be
perilous for England if *France* is the ally of England's enemies. Even
the attitude of America towards England would be more cautious than
it was in the Canada and Sackville affairs, if America had to rely on
carrying out a breach with England in isolation, and without any
moral or material help from France. There is no surer means of preventing America from relying on France in any quarrel with England
than the certainty that France would not be able to undertake an attack
on England without being herself attacked by a German army of over
a million. America will not be inclined to transmute her past ill-feeling
towards England and the chauvinistic tendencies of her future government into practical warfare, if it is not assured of eventual French
support. . . .

My idea is that, if His Majesty agrees, a treaty shall be concluded
between the English and German governments, by which each pledges
help to the other if France in the course of the next one, two, or three
years, as the case may be, should *attack* either power, and that this

treaty, which should be binding for the German Empire even without any parliamentary resolution, should be laid before the English parliament for approval, and presented openly to the German Reichstag.

I think that a bold and open step of this kind will have a calming effect and relieve tension not only in England and Germany but in the whole of Europe, and that it will establish the position of the English government as the protector of the peace of the world.

Owing to her predominantly maritime strength England needs now, just as much as she did in the last century, a continental ally, and this need, owing to the enormous increase in military armaments on the continent, is stronger now than it ever was. Without such an alliance there is always the possibility, with present-day communications, of a French invasion of England, depending on the vagaries of the weather, provocation, and the prevailing strength of striking power in the Channel. With an Anglo-German alliance France will not be in a position to plan an effective attack on England and at the same time the defence against a German attack on her eastern frontier.

In my opinion it would be of no advantage for England to pursue her policy of reserve so far that all the continental powers and especially Germany have to prepare for the safeguarding of their own future without relying on England. If we finally became convinced that England would continue to pursue this policy, then Germany would find it necessary to seek her own salvation in such international relations as it could achieve without England's participation. Such expedients, once adopted, are in politics not easy to undo. . . . I do not expect any immediate answer to this, but will wait for as long an interval as Lord Salisbury needs to determine his own view and that of his political colleagues, before reporting to my master the Emperor on the result.

GP, iv, no. 943

5   Bismarck's Reichstag Speech of 26 January 1889

I regard England as the old traditional ally, whose interests do not clash with ours; when I say 'ally', it is not to be construed in the diplomatic sense; we have no treaties with England;—but it is my desire to maintain the friendly relations we have had with England for the last 150 years, and in colonial questions too (Bravo! on the left). And if I had proof that we were in danger of losing them then I would become cautious and seek to avoid that loss. . . .

I am not one of those who, after the majority in parliament has decided to participate in something, persist in a petty and pernickety opposition, in order to prevent the majority from carrying out a policy they have already decided upon, and erect a stumbling-block (spirited applause on the right), and cannot stop proclaiming the fact that they are of a different opinion and set themselves in opposition to the whole country and its majority (applause on the right).

Under certain circumstances, as a minister, I can do that, if I fear, as was the case in the year 1862, that the majority in the country was moving in a dangerous direction; and I can do it, when I find myself as then opposed to the abdication document of my king and master, who says to me, 'Will you stand by me or shall I abdicate?' Then I can take action and oppose a whole sea of weapons. But for two million, or for Zanzibar, one cannot in my opinion go against the main stream of a national movement (Bravo! on the right); one cannot be petty and go on railing against something that has already been decided by the nation at large. I subordinate my views. I have never been a colonial man; I have had righteous scruples, and only the pressure of public opinion and of the majority view has made me decide to capitulate and defer to the opinions of others. And I would counsel that to Mr. Deputy Bamberger (Bravo! on the right); he has not yet the right, which I have after 26 years of service, to stand out against the whole country (vociferous applause on the right)....

GW, xiii, pp. 380, 382-4

6 Bismarck praises his own Moderation

Conversation with the editor Anton Memminger, at Kissingen, 16 August 1890

... Many people have already spoken of my political principles. The professors and their adherents in the newspapers are continually lamenting that I have not given them any clue to the principles which have guided my policy. The Germans, who have hardly emerged yet from the political nursery, cannot get accustomed to considering politics as a science of the possible, as my intimate opponent Pope Pius IX rightly described it. Politics are not like mathematics or arithmetic. It is true that in politics one has to calculate with known and unknown quantities at one and the same time, but there are no formulae or rules by which one can work out the answer in advance. Hence I have not adhered to the opinions and expedients of other statesmen, but have rather used their errors in calculation as a warning to myself. Napoleon I failed because, presuming on his military victories, he started quarrels with all the other countries instead of maintaining peace. Success in war made him arrogant and pugnacious. In his thirst for world domination he ran into endless dangers, which brought about his fall. His great achievement fell in ruins after a short time because he did not practise the first virtue of a statesman towards other nations—after great successes, wise moderation—and involved Europe in one war after another, whereas I myself after 1871 made every effort to maintain peace. And I did not consciously take up an opposite view only to Napoleon I, but also to Napoleon III. It is true that the latter strove only to imitate the more favourable attributes of his uncle; but in constantly trying, as the 'honest broker', to get some profit for himself, he fell into the habit, like those Italian diplomats of the last century, of confusing cunning with duplicity. I played my cards openly. I countered deliberate cunning with impressive truth. That they often did not believe me and afterwards felt surprised and hurt, was not my fault. . . .

GW, ix, pp. 93-4

7   The need for a German Hegemony in Europe

. . . It is our interest to maintain peace, while without exception our continental neighbours have wishes, either secret or officially avowed, which cannot be fulfilled except by war. We must direct our policy in accordance with these facts—that is, we must do our best to prevent war or limit it. . . .

Our non-interference cannot reasonably be directed to sparing our forces so as, after the others have weakened themselves, to fall upon any of our neighbours or a possible opponent. On the contrary, we ought to do all we can to weaken the bad feeling which has been called out through our growth to the position of a real Great Power, by honourable and peaceful use of our influence, and so convince the world that a German hegemony in Europe is more useful and less partisan and also less harmful for the freedom of others than that of France, Russia, or England. The respect for the rights of other states in which France especially has always been so wanting at the time of her supremacy, and which in England lasts only so long as English interests are not touched, is made easy for the German Empire and its policy, on one side owing to the practicality of the German character, on the other by the fact (which has nothing to do with our deserts) that we do not require an increase of our immediate territory, and also that we could not attain it without strengthening the centrifugal elements in our own territory. It has always been my ideal aim, after we had established our unity within the possible limits, to win the confidence not only of the smaller European states, but also of the Great Powers, and to convince them that German policy will be just and peaceful, now that it has repaired the *injuria temporum*, the disintegration of the nation. In order to produce this confidence it is above everything necessary that we should be honourable, open, and easily reconciled in case of friction or *untoward events*. I have followed this recipe not without some personal reluctance . . . and I imagine that in the future also opportunities will not be wanting of showing that we are appeased and peaceful. During the time that I was in office I advised three wars, the Danish, the Bohemian, and the French; but every time I first made myself clear whether the war, if it were successful, would bring a prize of victory worth the sacrifices which every war requires, and which now are so much greater than in the last century. . . .

R & R, ii, 287-90

SHORT LIST OF BOOKS FOR FURTHER READING

W. N. Medlicott, *Bismarck and Modern Germany* (1965: short introductory survey)

W. E. Mosse, *The European Powers and the German Question, 1848-1871* (1958)

O. Pflanze, *Bismarck and the Development of Germany: The Period of Unification, 1815-1871* (1963: this work, with Mosse's, gives a detailed general survey of the period to 1870)

C. W. Clark, *Franz Joseph and Bismarck* (1934)

L. D. Steefel, *The Schleswig-Holstein Question* (1932)

L. D. Steefel, *Bismarck, the Hohenzollern Candidacy, and the Origins of the Franco-German War of 1870* (1962)

W. L. Langer, *European Alliances and Alignments, 1871-1890* (1931: still the best of the more detailed surveys of the period after 1870)

F. Haselmayr, *Diplomatische Geschichte des Zweiten Reichs von 1871-1918* (the first three volumes (1955, 1956, 1957) give a competent survey of the period 1871-1890 for German readers)

W. Windelband, *Bismarck und die europäischen Grossmächte, 1879-1885* (1942)

W. N. Medlicott, *Bismarck, Gladstone, and the Concert of Europe* (1957)

M. E. Townshend, *The Rise and Fall of Germany's Colonial Empire, 1884-1918* (1942)

S. E. Crowe, *The Berlin West African Conference* (1942)

Hans Kohn (ed.), *German History, some new German Views* (1954)